HOW THE UNIVERSE WAS CREATED
AND OTHER USELESS FACTS

WILLOW SHIPPERLEY

How the Universe Was Created
And Other Useless Facts

WILLOW SHIPPERLEY

© 2015 by Willow Shipperley. All rights reserved.
Cover art by Irene Javier
ISBN-13: 978-1511476317
ISBN-10: 1511476311

Printed in the United States of America. No part of this book may be reproduced in any written, electronic, recording, or photocopying without express written permission of the author.

This is a work of fiction. Any names, characters, places, and incidents are coincidental and do not reflect the views of the author or publisher.

To all who are kind enough to pick up this book
and who take the time to laugh.

The Beginning of Everything

Before there was everything, there was nothing. Well, *mostly* nothing. It's nothing if you ignore all the stuff that was there in the void. But really, everybody just thought that there was nothing, at all! Sort of. Anyway, there was nothing until Commotus created light and everyone saw that there was a whole lot of something. Everything, in fact. In addition, as soon as there was light, there was sound, and with sound came the conflicting claims of everyone in existence that they themselves had created the universe.

The resulting argument sounded remarkably similar to one children might have when arguing over who had been playing with a toy first. The toy, in this instance, was everything in creation. While the children's – sorry, while the *gods'* – collective fury escalated, Commotus set about creating time. There is no real way to tell how long it took, because there was no way to measure time before its own creation, but the argument amongst the other gods had not moved past the "I was here first" screaming match by the time it did pop up. That could either be because Commotus is super powerful and creating everything was an instantaneous effort, or the other gods were just really single minded and hadn't bothered to look outside of their fury for a moment to see what he was doing. Either way, while Commotus was dancing around creating even *more* stuff to fill the not-void, like air, and things to stand on, the other gods did nothing but insist that they created everything.

After a while, the effects of the freshly created time began to drag on the gods' stamina, and half an aeon later, silence filled the not-void for the first time since it had been created. Commotus, who had not spoken up to that point, stepped into the mix, and the other gods focused their attentions on him.

"This is chaos!" he laughed.

"Hey!" One shouted, "You're the guy who turned on the light!"

"Am I?" Commotus replied, with a grin that flashed rows of light-year long teeth.

"Yeah, you are!" Another one piped up. The Nameless Gods encircled Commotus, their fury quickly bubbling over again.

Commotus only shrugged in reply. The gods then leaped at him in one wrathful wave, blindly attempting to destroy him. At this time, it is apt to mention that because of a rather significant size difference between Commotus and the Nameless Gods, the attack was something similar to dust motes floating gently towards the Earth.

"Take us back to the void!" they howled, "Turn off the light!" Commotus, being the Really Cool Dude he was, understood that the gods needed to feel like they were singular beings, capable of creating entire universes.

The Beginning of Everything

With another large smile, he created a multitude of puncture holes in the not-void, creating miniscule pockets that would be as airless, groundless, soundless, and lightless as the void had been. The black pinpricks each swallowed a Nameless God, and around them exploded large star patterns which contained the groups of rocks and gases that make up what modern scientists call "galaxies."

Immediately, the furious complaints ceased, and the not-void was silent. Commotus watched the black holes as some of the more volatile gods attempted to wipe each other out, and tracked the progress of the others as they tried to move as far away from each other as possible. He was content to sit and watch the other gods for a bit over nine billion years before it occurred to him that he could make another, empty pinprick to represent himself in the antics.

The idea took over his thoughts as he went along to direct the formation of small rock bits to orbit the superheated balls of gas that circled his new black hole. Eventually, he became so enthralled with this pinprick that he forgot to pay attention to the others all together. Commotus rooted for one rock in particular, in the same way a person will arbitrarily pick a car to cheer for when someone puts on NASCAR and there's nothing else to do but watch it. This small rocky bit, he decided, was to be the home for the first of the creatures which he would create.

Thus was the creation of the Universe.

Willow Shipperley

The First Beings of the Rock

The first thing Commotus did to the rock was give it a core of fire. It reminded him of the stars that made up his being, and those that surrounded the black holes containing the Nameless Gods. The outside of the rock was then coated in water, and green leafy things sprouted up to create a single, enormous landmass. Immediately afterwards, Commotus discovered that along with the creation of these three things had been the creation of three corresponding entities. Not surprisingly, their personalities were linked to the matter that they represented, and before Commotus could speak, they had declared names for themselves.

"I am a powerful and angry god," the spirit of the fire core roared. "My name shall be Infearno, and all who hear it will cower before me!"

"My name is William," the water spirit said simply, looking directly at Commotus.

"And I," began the third spirit grandly, "Am the God of Everything Living and Beautiful and… Stuff."

Commotus nodded towards the miniscule spirits as

they stood on the rock, acknowledging their claims. He then sat silently for a time, and watched the three interact amongst themselves. Already, Infearno was trying to assert dominance over the other two spirits.

"Your name is too long!" he shouted at the God of Everything Living and Beautiful and Stuff. "I'm going to call you... GELBS!"

"What? That's a horrible name!" she cried in reply.

"Is not!"

"Is too!

"Well, you're the one who made it in the first place!" Infearno screamed.

The argument quickly dissolved as anger caused Infearno's flaming form to heat up. GELBS immediately caught fire and began panicking, and Commotus watched with curiosity as she crumpled to ash and slowly regrew back to her original form. William, on the other hand, calmly ignored both Infearno and The God of Everything Living and Beautiful and Stuff, acting only to avoid the conflict between the two.

"Spirits," Commotus called after a time. "I wish to know your thoughts on something. If you were to create a completely new being, how would you style its form?"

"That's easy!" Shouted Infearno. "It would be large, and all consuming, and be yellow and orange and red!"

"I think something winding, and ever growing would do wonderfully," GELBS said.

"I think a being which has no set form, and can change with any situation would be nice," William said.

Commotus nodded again, and the three spirits went

back to their mostly harmless bickering. Each of the three spirits had described creatures that reflected themselves, and suddenly he knew that the first creatures he made to live on the rock would be created after an image of himself. The structure he designed was where most similarity lay – the first of the creatures had a long, elegant neck, a tail of matching length, and a sturdy body. However, the creature had four stubby legs instead of six, to better walk the land with, and its skin was fluffy and white. Just because these creatures would be made in his image didn't mean they could handle being made of stars, like he was. Once he was sure that his first creature was perfect, he moved on, making a powerful creature that balanced on its back legs and had oddly small arms, and many others with a variety of tail lengths, jaw sizes, and appetites. All of them had the same fluffy white skin as the first.

    A large majority were placed in the waters too deep for the green leafy things to grow, although a portion of them remained on land. After letting them loose, Commotus watched with pride as the one which most closely resembled him moved through its daily activities of walking, eating, and sleeping. However, it was not long before the pleasant atmosphere on the rock was shattered by a heated argument between Infearno and The God of Everything Living and Beautiful and Stuff. It quickly proved itself to be so disruptive that all the creatures – including Commotus's personal favorite – had to move farther and farther away from the spirits, until they were all pushed up to the water's edge. This, in turn made

Commotus angry, because he had never really meant for the spirits to be created, and yet there they were, taking up space and destroying things. Commotus confronted the two spirits, using a tone reminiscent of the Nameless Gods, and asked them what it was they thought they were doing.

"I want more land," Infearno said.

At the same time, The God of Everything Living and Beautiful and Stuff explained, "He's destroying everything and attacking me needlessly!"

Commotus regarded them and their answers for a moment, before replying, "Infearno, I created the land you wish to take *for* the beautiful creatures which you have displaced. You must return to your home inside the rock and allow them to return to theirs."

"But The God of Everything Living and Beautiful and Stuff is allowed to be up here!" Infearno protested. Commotus was growing impatient, because as long as he was in this conversation, he could not watch over and protect his dinosaurs.

"The God of Everything Living and Beautiful and Stuff is not trying to *take over* the land that she already *lives in* – she is merely trying to keep everything in good working order so my beautiful creatures have a place to live and be happy. Now go." Infearno sank through the ground with Commotus's final words, leaving a singed and deadened patch of grass that GELBS knew she could not fix. Slowly, the dinosaurs returned to the land and resumed their slow, happy lives.

This stretch of time lasted many years, during which

The First Beings of the Rock

Commotus freely interacted with his beloved creatures, and the sun existed in the night sky, creating a perpetual day time. It was merely a blip on the scale Commotus was planning on spending with the dinosaurs, but one day, the large mounds of rock that William had been eating away at exploded, and out of them came a slow but deadly liquid fire that appeared to be inescapable. Rising into the air with a thick cloud of ash, Commotus found Infearno, back and stronger than ever.

"Fear me!" he roared, as more and more of the lava spilled from the broken rock mounds. "I am Infearno, God of Fire, and all who hear my name shall bow before me!"

Commotus was shocked, to say the least. It was a good hour before he was able to get past the horror of watching his beautiful creatures all succumb to the superheated rock sludge to address the spirit.

"What are you doing?"

"What does it look like?" Infearno grinned at the god of creation, his flickering, flame-like body causing his smile to stretch and contort disturbingly.

"It looks like you are ending the collective existence of all of my creatures."

"A side effect!"

"Of?"

"My taking over the rock and making the outside look like the inside."

Many thoughts were racing through Commotus's mind. Most concerned the fate of his creatures, but a part of him was starting to worry about the fate of the rock.

The fire core was important; it kept the rock at a livable temperature for his creatures, and it gave it a spark of life. However, the rest of the planet was also part of a delicate balance. The green leafy things were vital to the survival of the rock and the creatures on it, and the vast bodies of water were home to more life than anywhere else. As the fire grew bigger and bigger, the water and the green leafy things grew smaller and smaller, until they were down to singular quantities of both. Commotus knew that he couldn't explain this to Infearno; although he claimed to be a god, he was weak and small. Even the Nameless Gods would have towered over him. He was simply too small to understand something so big.

Two problems had arisen from this challenge to his power – well, three, if the destruction of all living creatures counted. One, Commotus was too big to simply destroy Infearno; if he tried, the end result would be No More planet. Two, Commotus was a being of Creation, and as such was unable to destroy anything, even if he had wanted to. This left him with only one plan of action.

The first thing he needed to do was stop Infearno. The only two things left that could possibly push him back to the core were the two spirits that had been created beside him, William and the God of Everything Living and Beautiful and Stuff. The two needed no encouragement to bring Infearno down. The God of Everything Living and Beautiful and Stuff quickly got over her hesitation to hurt anything living in order to avenge those who had been destroyed, and William proved her strength by rearing up high above the rock.

The First Beings of the Rock

So, while The God of Everything Living and Beautiful and Stuff distracted Infearno through taunts and jabs, William gathered herself and in one giant wave swallowed the entire rock in water. When she retreated, all of the creatures had been buried under the stone, and Infearno was as small as a candle flame. He didn't need to be told when he was beat, and sank down through the land until he reached the core once again.

Commotus aided the God of Everything Living and Beautiful and Stuff in regrowing all the green leafy things, and settled William down in a ditch where she could recover her strength and spread out. Small parts of her were left all over the rock, forming the basis of the many streams, lakes, and underground reservoirs to be discovered later. Commotus knew he had to salvage the remains of his beautiful creatures, but they were too firmly fused to the rock to simply pull out. Leaving the bones behind turned out to be the only way to safely remove his beautiful creatures from the new layer of rock. The fluffy white exteriors would not be able to survive if they were actually near Commotus, so he compromised by suspending them above the rock, high above the ground, where they remained indefinitely.

Thus was the creation of clouds.

Willow Shipperley

The King Who Wanted Everything to Be On Fire

It was not very long after the destruction of the dinosaurs that Commotus found himself thinking about creating again. It was a part of his nature that would not allow itself to be ignored. He floundered around for a while, unsure how to continue. He felt so sad without his dinosaurs, but he knew he couldn't remain wallowing in grief forever. The god of creation decided that the new beings would not be made in his image; he didn't want to cheapen the memory of his favorite creatures by simply replacing them. No, the new creatures would have to look completely different. They would be smaller, for one, without tails and with stubby teeth. Commotus made many of these new creatures, dubbing them the Humans, before continuing and creating other creatures, until it seemed that the rock was filled with them.

The entire process took around twenty minutes, give or take. Immediately after finishing, the creatures all awoke and set about exploring. Most had been placed by Commotus only in certain areas, like forests, deserts, or water; the Humans, on the other hand, had been scattered all across the rock. This caused the immediate death of many Humans, as they awoke submerged in the deepest waters and suspended from the highest heights. Luckily, Commotus had made many more Humans than other creatures, because without any sort of template to work from, there had been a lot of trial and error before an acceptable model was created. However, those that remained living quickly found each other, and most of the other creatures followed suit.

All the creatures shared the desire to survive. It was the basis of their creation, and it linked all of them in a way that excluded Commotus, who could not die. The concept of being alive and then not being alive was something he didn't quite understand. The creature which Commotus most identified with, and rooted for, was what later would be called the giraffe, because it looked a bit like him. This creature, and many others, turned to the green and leafy things he'd provided to stay alive. However, to his horror, many of his beautiful little creatures turned to each other for food.

The first time darkness obscured the sun was terrifying for all. While some creatures found themselves functioning better without light, most were left defenseless and terrified that the light would never return. The Humans were particularly useless. In the darkness they could not see, and they did not have any natural weapons – no claws, nor teeth, nor wings to keep predators away. Many died in the darkness, killed by the creatures who hungered for blood. When, by miracle of miracles, the ball of light did return to the black sky, the humans found that they were not much safer. After many cycles of the light and dark, even the weakest of other creatures had found a pattern on the rock, something to keep them safe – except for the humans. They were out of place amongst the dangers, and found safety only in numbers. Until, during one time of darkness, a Human who none of the others had ever seen before mysteriously joined their ranks.

"Greetings, humans," he boomed, with a large smile. The others stared at him, wary and silent. He carried a smell unlike anything they had sensed before, but that did not stop it from setting off warning after warning in their minds. The word "danger" took on a new meaning, fused with a fear of something they just couldn't quite remember. Taking the silence for suspicion, the man spoke again, in the loud voice that attracted enemies. "I am *also* a human," he declared.

"Who are you?" asked one muscular human.

The man's smile slipped into a smirk briefly. "Someone who can help," he replied. "I have something that can make you powerful, and set you apart from all the other creatures."

"What is this thing?" asked the same human.

After a slight pause, during which the man turned a toothy grin towards the starry night sky, he lifted a single, glowing finger to eye level, and whispered, "Fire."

The danger warning in the humans' minds escalated to a frantic shout, but as Commotus would find to be the case with humanity for most of their time on the rock, the promise of power and control was enough to override the warning, which was then dismissed with all the care and attention to detail as of someone agreeing to a website's "Terms and Conditions."

"We gladly accept your help," the human said with a grin.

"Very well," the strange man said, lowering his flickering hand. "What shall I call you?"

Looking around at the land, the human noted with surprise that the darkness of night was already beginning to fade, without a single casualty. The start of a promising day filled the human's head, and it replied happily, "You can call me Dawn."

"Okay, Dawn," the man said, shifting his gaze to include the rest of the wide-eyed, silent humans. "You can call me King."

Commotus, who up until this point had been checking out the living arrangement of the Nameless Gods (all of whom were still fighting to be the creator) did not at first notice anything odd about the strange man, other than that he didn't remember creating him. Everyone else was very distinctly alive; he could see a small portion of the glittering, colorful beings that they were underneath the physical body in everyone except the man.

The level of structure and order the pack of humans had was unusual, and hadn't existed before the strange man had arrived. All of the other humans seemed to be taking orders from him, and – was that *fire* he saw? Indeed it was, and Commotus's heart sank when he saw that they were carrying it on sticks and using it to chase

The King Who Wanted Everything to Be On Fire

away other creatures. He could feel their raw terror as they ran farther and farther into the land where the God of Everything Living and Beautiful and Stuff lived.

"King," one of the humans said. The man turned to face it, and Commotus watched, curious and confused.

"Yes, Dawn?"

"We have done as you asked. All of the creatures have been driven back past the large rock mounds."

"Very good," the man, King, said.

"Thank you for your help," it replied.

"Oh, I'm not done yet, Dawn," King replied. Commotus felt a growing sense of dread drop like a peach pit in his chest.

"The humans are safe now, what more is there to do?" Dawn asked.

"You are safe *for now*, but what if a creature decides to fight back when the idea of fire is no longer new?"

Dawn's eyes widened in renewed fear. "What can we do?"

"We're going to have to set everything on fire," King replied gravely.

"Yes, of course!" Dawn replied. The human turned and sped off to spread the message.

Commotus could not do anything to stop his creatures as they spread the deadly flame through all variety of green leafy things. However, he was able to warn the God of Everything Living and Beautiful and Stuff of the oncoming danger before the humans reached her.

Dawn approached first, leading the rest of the pack,

and was greeted by what seemed to be a living, moving, green leafy thing.

"Mortal humans," it said, with a voice like wind through tree branches. "I am the God of Everything Living and Beautiful and Stuff."

"And I am Dawn. Do you stand in our way with our mission of fire?"

"Oh, no, nothing like that," she replied. "In fact, I want to help you. Let me take care of setting all the trees on fire, alright?"

Dawn nodded. "Thank you for your help," it said, and the pack left.

Immediately, the God of Everything Living and Beautiful and Stuff began painting the leaves of the trees red, orange, and yellow – the colors of fire. Not too long after, King strolled through, and appeared to be satisfied. He was glowing orange throughout his whole body now, as opposed to just his finger. The God of Everything Living and Beautiful and Stuff hid from him, but followed him until he left the dense, not-really-on-fire forest. When he was gone, she looked up to the sky, and confirmed Commotus's fears.

"That's Infearno in human form," she said. Commotus then sought out William, who was steadily carving out a rather grand canyon. She was more than happy to help put the fire spirit back in his place, so Commotus stepped in front of the sun, plunging the world into a sudden night, and watched as slowly, the red-orange glow of the rock faded into darkness.

With the fire extinguished, the Humans found that

The King Who Wanted Everything to Be On Fire

their King not only wasn't glowing, but was also starting to lose his human-like form. Dawn threw herself down in front of his disintegrating form, which turned to ash and left only a candle flame on the ground.

"Fear me!" he squeaked. "I am Infearno, god of fire!"

"Go home," Dawn whispered.

With another pitiful "fear me," Infearno sunk into the ground without leaving a mark.

The next day, the creatures of the rock were all awoken by the howling scream of the God of Everything Living and Beautiful and Stuff.

"My trees! My beautiful, leafy trees!" she wailed. Looking over at the forests, Commotus saw that all the plants which had been painted to trick Infearno no longer looked vibrant and fire-like. Instead, the leaves were all shriveled and brown. Many of them had already fallen off, and lay in piles on the ground. With the sudden lack of heat from the fires, the rock took on a frosty quality, and it was months before Commotus was able to aid the God of Everything Living and Beautiful and Stuff in regrowing green leafy things.

Surprisingly, the next year the same thing happened – the trees had learned this behavior and retained it even in the depths of the cold. The practice continues on to this day, where at the end of the heat that signifies Infearno's plotting, the leaves will protect themselves from his rage with their bright, fiery colors.

Thus was the creation of autumn.

Willow Shipperley

The Cube

Something was wrong with the creatures on the rock. It had been many years, but there was the same number living as there had been when Commotus first created them. This wouldn't have been odd, except for the fact that many had died during the nights, during Infearno's second failed takeover, and in accidents with breathing water and falling off of tall things. The creatures had begun to converse freely with Commotus, which delighted him immensely, but no one would tell him how they were all still alive. One human offered to destroy itself, so that Commotus might watch and find out what was happening, and reluctantly he agreed.

The human chose to drop into a volcano, and Commotus felt an immense sadness. Even knowing that it would return completely intact, he knew that he had not created beautiful creatures for them to happily destroy themselves. As the human's body disintegrated, Commotus caught a breathtaking view of its essence, its spirit. It had a shapeless, flickering form, and it was constantly growing. It was the purest essence of life; the base upon which everything was created. As it rose from the depths of Infearno's lair, it caught the light of the sun and shimmered like the most perfectly cut diamond. Gathering speed, it quickly left the rock and, to Commotus's surprise, set itself on a direct path to the black hole.

Commotus had a hard time following the beautiful spirit as it disappeared into the pinprick, but he was able to look inside well enough. Inside was a massive pool of glittering spirits, spinning slowly around a cube that seemed to float in the center. Commotus was stunned, because he knew without a doubt that he had not created it, and yet it glowed and shimmered in the same way everything else did.

The spirit of the human, which had disappeared into the dazzling spiral for a moment, resurfaced and spiraled closer and closer to the cube until the fuzzy edges of its existence reached its angular sides. Some measure of the light inside the cube was absorbed by the spirit, and with a renewed glow it dove back into the lazily circling crowd. It began to speed up imperceptibly, moving faster and faster until it was zipping along the edge of the black hole's event horizon, and then, faster than the speed of light it shot back out into space, heading directly for the rock.

Commotus just barely caught the movement with his eye, but he was able to follow the beautiful soul all the way back to the volcano where its body had been destroyed. There was a flash of light, and then – to his horror – the original broken body of the human climbed over the edge of the volcano and tumbled down into the

The Cube

grass below. It glowed unnaturally, almost as if the sun had been placed inside of it. The sun, or the cube, which glowed just as bright. Flesh rapidly attached itself back to bones as they formed, until the human's body was complete and the glow diminished.

Sitting up, it smiled up towards Commotus. "See?"

Commotus nodded, a jerky gesture. "Go home to your friends," he said. The human cheerfully turned to go, before Commotus spoke again. "Wait, human. What is your name?"

"I have no name."

"Everyone has a name, even if they do not know it."

"Do you know it?"

Commotus was silent for a moment as he tried to see the name of the human. He turned his mind away from the rest of the rock's creatures, stopped monitoring the paths of the Nameless Gods, and focused his complete attention on the human before him. "You are Simon, the Listener."

"Thank you," Simon said, smiling up toward the god of creation. Commotus felt an odd feeling, similar to the one that used to overwhelm him when he would watch his favorite dinosaur complete even a simple activity. It was like love, but it had overtones of pity, and it showed him just how big the gap was between him and his creations. There were so many things they didn't know, that they would never know. Things they must be protected from.

Simon was still standing where he'd been before Commotus had started thinking about his emotions, only now he was staring at a leaf.

"Go home," Commotus whispered.

"Alright," he replied, and disappeared into the trees. Commotus hastily resumed scanning the not-void for threats to his pinprick, but luckily all other Nameless Gods were still too busy pretending that they were singular creation gods in a void to try and take over anywhere else. For a while after Commotus's conversation with the human ended, he dawdled around, trying to come up with a reason to allow his creatures to be undead and "live" happily forever. He didn't.

Eventually, Commotus journeyed back over to the pinprick which was the center of his galaxy. The cube, and the spirits swirling around it, were still as dazzling and bright as ever. Commotus felt rather strange in the presence of something which he most definitely did not remember creating. It didn't even *look* like anything he'd created. This cube was smooth and symmetrical, whereas everything Commotus had given life to was rough and organic.

"Hello, cube," he said. The spirits stirred, circling faster for a few moments before settling down again in their lazy spiral. The cube did not reply. "Something is wrong with my creatures, and I think you are a part of it. Survival is their first function, but with you here, no one is surviving. They just keep decomposing and recomposing, which isn't the same thing."

Commotus watched as a flurry of about twenty spirits launched themselves from the rock and joined the pool of glittering ethereal bodies. Many more back on the planet were ignoring dangers like other creatures eating them and not being able to survive being on fire, and at the same time holding one-sided conversations with the sky where they though Commotus was.

"I think I'm a part of it, too. My creatures can't be who I made them to be if they know about you and me." The cube continued to glow, and the spirits one by one filled themselves with its light before launching back towards the rock. "I have to take away their knowledge of me, and make them completely independent, don't I?" The cube did not respond.

Upon returning to the rock, Commotus called upon the three spirits. "I have a mission for all of you."

"A mission? Doing what?" Asked the God of Everything Living and Beautiful and Stuff.

"I need you to kill every creature on the rock."

The God of Everything Living and Beautiful and Stuff gasped, while the other two spirits sat in stunned silence.

"When I inconvenienced your first creatures you were furious. Now you're *asking* me to *destroy* your second batch?" Infearno asked.

"Yes. But please, do not make it hurt. I don't want to put them through any distress, I just need to remove all of their spirits and I can't personally do it without destroying you three."

"Okay," said William. "When do we start?"

"In just a minute. Hold on." Commotus searched the forests hurriedly until he came across Simon attempting to catch a fish by himself.

"Oh, hello Commotus," the human said cheerfully when he noticed the god of creation's presence.

"Simon, I need to tell you something, and I want you to take my message to everyone."

"Okay, but couldn't you tell them yourself? It wouldn't take very long-"

"I can't today, Simon. I have to do something important."

A confused look dropped onto Simon's face, and was wiped away as fast as a windshield wiper would slick rain off of a car, replaced immediately with unquestioning trust. "What do you want me to tell everyone?"

"Tell them that I, Commotus, god of creation, love each and every creature that I have created. Do not be afraid of what is happening around you, and know that I am doing it for your own good. Things are going to be very different soon, and I want you to live and love to the best of your ability, although you will not remember-"

"FIFTY-NINE, SIXTY! Come on guys, it's time to KILL EVERYONE!" Infearno charged into the clearing and turned Simon into a pile of ash before charging toward his village. The God of Everything Living and Beautiful and Stuff followed after, whooping, and William surged by in a stream.

"-me," Commotus ended. The image of Simon's trusting face half-turned to a scream was imprinted in his mind, and the warm feelings of compassion he'd been fostering with his speech were frozen and brittle. For a brief second he considered annihilating Infearno for daring to destroy Simon, but he knew it would make no difference. He knew that what he needed to do was more important than his feelings, and he could explain to the over-excited spirit what a figure of speech was later.

Moving to look into the pinprick, Commotus watched the steady flow of spirits as they moved from their rock and into the pocket of void all at once. Some were already reaching for the Cube, but as more and more spirits tried to reach it, the less it seemed to shine. When at last every creature from the rock was spinning inside the black hole that was his pinprick, Commotus spoke.

"My beautiful creatures, I know that you are scared. I can feel it." The spirits stirred slightly at his voice before returning to their slow spinning. "What I am going to do will allow you to fully experience what it means to be alive. Keep your fear close, for it is a part of your experience, but keep your curiosity closer." Commotus gently pulled the Cube away from the spirits. "This is the same essence of creation which I hold inside of me. I give it to each of you, so that you and I can be the same." The spirits stirred again, trying to move towards the god of creation, but without the light of the Cube they were not strong enough. "As a final measure, to make sure that you truly move along your own paths, I remove your knowledge of me."

Commotus bit down on the Cube, shattering it. The light streamed into the black hole, and lit up every spirit within. With the light of creation inside them, the creatures gathered speed and shot themselves back to the rock, reforming their bodies one last time.

Moving back to face his rock, he watched as his creatures picked themselves up and began moving as if nothing had happened. Some creatures moved in packs, and some moved alone. The humans were his biggest puzzle. Almost immediately, they began to give names to other creatures, and themselves. The names they came up with did not match the spirits inside them.

Dawn was very vocal in this naming ceremony. "My name is Adam," she said. Pointing to a large human, who was very busy watching the darkening sky, she said "Your name will be Eve."

"No," the human responded with a frown. "No, my name is Simon."

Thus it is shown where we go when we die.

The Intention of the Universe

For a while after Commotus erased himself from the minds of all his creatures, he didn't know what to do. He'd never before had such an urge to speak, or otherwise make himself known. Before, if he wanted to help out a rabbit, or advise a human, all he had to do was lean down and start talking. It wasn't until now that the opportunity was gone that he realized just how important the small interactions could be. So what could he do but sit and watch?

Eventually, Commotus could no longer stand to watch his creations and feel their emotions, so upset he was with his own situation. So, he took a walk to clear his head – or, rather, he took a "float," since he wasn't necessarily walking through the not-void. Changing directions only to avoid the small pinpricks that contained the Nameless Gods, the god of creation soon found himself so far away from his creations that when he looked over his shoulder he was only just able to see the local group that contained their galaxy.

He continued until he passed the edge of what scientists would one day call the "Virgo Supercluster," which as they defined it was a mass concentration of groups of galaxies. Beyond it were many more galaxies, whose light would not reach earth for many billions of years. Or, that's what *should* have been there. Instead, all Commotus could see was an opaque darkness which he had definitely not put there. Was this another thing that had been created by some being other than him?

Commotus slowly floated closer to the darkness, curious to examine its physical properties. However, it seemed that the closer he got to it, the farther away the center appeared to be. The god of creation felt deeply unsettled by this odd development, which looked as though it might stretch to the end of the universe. None of the stars or galaxies which he had created were visible. Deciding to return later, after he'd had some time to think about what this *thing* could possibly be, Commotus turned around and began to head back. At least, that's what he'd intended to do. Unfortunately, everything behind him was just as dark as everything that had been in front of him. Immediately the unsettled feeling he'd been fostering intensified, and a shiver danced its way down his spine. What *was* this? It certainly wasn't something of his own design – he would remember creating a dark, light swallowing mist. Wouldn't he? When he'd seen the cube, the differences between it and his own creations was startlingly clear. Where his creatures were always asymmetrical and organic, warm with life, the cube was sharp and clean cut, and its light was cold.

This dark mist was much more similar to his creations; it was organic, and as far as he could tell it didn't have much of a shape at all. However, like the cube, it was cold, the way an icy breeze feels on bare skin after surfacing from a body of water. When Commotus tried to move in the direction he thought was forward, he found that his limbs were sluggish, and slow to respond to his commands. That definitely was not right. The god of creation should not be brought down by any physical conditions. As far as he could tell, he could not be hurt, and he could not die. Yet, the cold that was seeping into his body seemed to say otherwise. The more Commotus struggled, the more helpless he began to feel. Was this what it felt like for his creatures to die? It seemed his panic was the same as theirs, so maybe the physical feelings were similar as well. The cold entered the edges of his mind like a light fog, slowing down his thoughts until it seemed he'd been swallowed whole.

"Commotus, it is important that you return to your creatures." The voice cut through the fog in the god's mind, jolting him awake enough to jerk his head around, looking for the speaker.

"Where-" he began, but his mouth and brain were still too frozen to form sentences.

"I do not have a physical form, but that is not important right now. For the time being, all you need to concern yourself with is returning to your creatures."

"I can't," Commotus whispered.

"Of course you can. You are the god of creation, one of the only true gods of this universe. You can do anything."

"How?" The longer the two spoke, the more

Commotus could feel and move his body.

"There is only one thing that I will ever tell you how to do, and it is not how to escape this being."

"Who are you? And what do you mean 'this being'? Is this darkness alive?" The voice did not reply. "Okay, great," Commotus grumbled to himself. What was it that he'd been told to do? Return to his creatures? Commotus hesitated, unsure if he should attempt to go back to a place where no one even knew he was missing. Honestly, it's not like anyone would miss him; only the three Spirits on earth were able to talk to him, and he was pretty sure that they would rather pretend they were the gods of the planet then come look for him.

A small part of him protested the negative train of thought. How could he leave his beloved creations all alone, scattered across the universe with the Nameless Gods? The answer was that he couldn't. He loved his creatures too much to leave them alone, even if they didn't know he existed. Maybe he could one day find a soul or two who were strong enough to handle knowing him, and who might remember some of their past lives. If Simon proved able to remember his true name, given to him by Commotus himself, then maybe he wouldn't have to do much searching after all. The voice was right; he needed to return to his creatures. The only question was how. He could freely move his limbs again, and could no longer feel the cold of the darkness surrounding him, but he had no idea which way to go.

Closing his many eyes, Commotus tried to focus on the emotions of his creatures. It took a while, but eventually he was able to locate the faintest, thinnest thread of emotion – all that was connecting him to those he had created. Turning back and forth, Commotus tried to locate the strongest path of the emotion, but it wasn't strong enough to pinpoint in any one direction.

"Voice!" Commotus called out, "Is there anything I can do to make the emotion-connection-thing stronger?"

"Yes," came the reply.

"Will you tell me what to do?" Commotus asked. The uneasiness radiating from the darkness was beginning to get to him again, strengthening his urge to leave as soon as possible.

There was a thoughtful pause. "No."

Commotus was becoming frustrated. "Well, can you give me a hint at least?" he growled.

"Yes – the light which shines within you can always light your path," the voice said. If Commotus hadn't been so frustrated by how difficult the voice was being, he might have noticed the pride with which it presented its clue.

"What does that even mean, 'the light that shines within'?" Commotus muttered. Was he supposed to take that literally? Of course, being practically made of stars did lend to him shining quite brightly in dark places, but that was external. So, metaphorical light? Could his godly grace make the connection between this almost non-existent emotion and himself stronger? Well, it was worth a shot.

Closing his eyes again, the god of creation focused solely on himself and the emotion, which he viewed in his head as a glowing string connecting him to his creatures. Channeling his creative energy into this string, he imagined it growing bigger and bigger, until the emotion was amped up to the max. Opening his eyes, he was disappointed to see that there was no brightly glowing path waiting for him. In addition, the emotion still felt incredibly weak.

"Oh, come on!" Commotus cried. "Voice, your hint was not helpful at all."

"Well, then you must be interpreting it wrong. Although, watching you concentrate was quite, uh, thrilling."

"Wait," Commotus said, temporarily forgetting his frustrations. "You can see me?"

"Of course I can see you," the voice scoffed.

"Are you stuck here as well, and just pretending to be helping me?" Commotus asked with dismay.

"Well, no. As I said later – I mean, earlier – I do not have a physical form. I can't be trapped by physical things."

Commotus paused when he heard the voice trip up. That didn't really match up with the super-intelligent, all-knowing image it had set up for itself earlier. "Voice, do you have a name?"

There was a long pause before the voice replied, "Yes."

"Can I know it?"

"It changes in each reincarnation, but I believe you named me Time in this universe," the voice said slowly.

"Time? Are you a Spirit?" Commotus asked in mixed

shock and dismay. If this being really was a spirit, there was no way it could help him. That would be the same as having Infearno trying to give him directions on how to escape a galactic tsunami.

"When I was first created, I was indeed a Spirit. However, I have been around for so long that I have become a god."

"Well, you can't have been around for longer than me, since I created you. What makes you an expert on me, then?" Commotus asked.

"I was the first thing you created – ever. However, I do not believe this conversation will lead to you returning to your creatures, so perhaps you should work on figuring a way out of here," Time said stiffly.

"Hold on a minute, the first thing I created was light, not time. Or do you not count anything that came before you?"

"This discussion should not be continued until earlier – I mean later, much, much later – and I very much want this to be a long-lasting universe, so I'm going to speed this up and get you back to your creatures now, okay?"

"Wait, what?" Commotus began, but before he could finish speaking, a blinding light began to shine from within him, blinding him. Then, as if amplified by the sheer brightness of it, the faint emotion connecting him to his creatures blazed to life, and began tugging him back towards creation. Quickly he slipped from the dark fog, and the farther he got from it, the less unsettled he felt. Before he could blink, he found himself back at earth, and was pleased to see that all of his creatures were getting along quite pleasantly; even the Spirits seemed to be in harmony.

The longer he watched his creatures, however, the more and more he found his mind drifting to his odd conversation with Time. The way it talked about the universe as if it was some temporary thing made no sense at all – there definitely hadn't been anything there *before* he created the universe. It was almost as if Time had existed throughout multiple universes, but if that was true, then it would be older than its creator, which definitely didn't make sense. Although Commotus knew that the Spirit was probably just trying to sound important, some part of him couldn't shake the feeling that there was truth in what it had said.

"Commotus," called GELBS, breaking his train of thought.

"Yes, what is it?" he replied, looking down towards the Spirit.

"Where have you been? We missed you," she said.

"Oh, nowhere, really. I was just visiting some of my other worlds," Commotus said with a weak smile.

"Can you talk to the creatures on those other planets?"

"No. Everything I created has forgotten me, no exceptions."

"Well that can't be true, since you're able to talk to me!" GELBS said cheerfully. "So, at least you have us Spirits to talk to."

Commotus considered explaining to the happy earth

spirit that actually, they *weren't* his creatures, they were simply mistakes resulting from his creation of the elements, but kept the thought to himself. Just because he was unhappy didn't mean that he had to bring everyone else down with him. Instead, he just smiled again, and said, "Of course. I don't know what I'd do without you three." GELBS beamed up at him like a proud child, and a wave of guilt sunk through him. The Spirits were a mistake, but that didn't mean he had to love them any less than he loved the rest of his creatures.

"Um, Commotus?" GELBS said, once again distracting him from his musings.

"Yes, GELBS?"

"Why has it become so hard to see you?"

Confused, Commotus glanced around. Was he not glowing as brightly as usual? Suddenly, a cold chill swept up his tail and back. Turning around, he saw nothing but darkness – no planets, no stars, no Nameless Gods. Moving to face his favorite planet again, Commotus was shocked to see that it, too, had been swallowed by darkness. Again Commotus began to feel unsettled. The fog had followed him.

"GELBS, are you still there?" He called out.

Very faintly, he heard a muffled reply: "What's going on?"

Commotus did not have an answer for her. Is this why Time had said it was so important to get back to his creatures? Not that he was any help, since all he'd done last time was glow a lot. Before he could call out to Time, and try to get some kind of help for his creatures, he realized that he felt more settled than he had a few moments ago. The nervous, fluttery, dismayed feeling that had come with the fog was leaving! A few moments later, the galaxies making up his universe were back.

"Oh, thank Me," the god of creation cried with a smile. It was clear that the fog had only been passing through, and was now headed away from his favorite creatures for good. Something still felt off, though. As he searched nervously for whatever had been changed, his eyes strayed to earth. A low-lying black fog lay invisible at the feet of his creatures, clinging to them as they walked, and sinking into the plants and meats they ate. Commotus watched in horror as countless creatures — humans and animals alike — began to die from poisons and ailments he'd never seen before. Although he'd never seen anything like this before, and definitely had not created the sicknesses that seemed to plague his creatures by the thousands now, he knew somewhere in his mind what this was. Disease.

"Who created this horrible thing?" Commotus whispered to himself.

"You, of course," Time whispered back. Commotus wondered for a second how long it had been there before turning his full attention back to his creatures.

"I would never," he growled, baring his teeth. Already he had created a form of protection, which he blew from his mouth to coat the planet. A light mist, it followed the path of the fog, sinking into the bodies of his creatures. "This creation, which shall be known as Immunity, will protect my creatures. Why would I create something that would hurt them and then create something else to combat it?"

"You aren't combating it. You are simply making it more complex."

Commotus snarled, and wished that Time had a physical form so he would have something to glare at. "You make no sense."

"You set the intention of the universe with your first words. Do you remember what they were?" Commotus thought back to The Beginning. *Did* he remember? Time didn't wait for him to answer. "This is a chaos universe."

"And the fog is, what, then?"

"That is Chaos."

"Is it a Spirit? Is it alive?" Commotus was nearly petrified with fear. Would this never end?

"It is the physical embodiment of the universe – not a Spirit, but definitely alive."

"Will it ever go away?" Commotus asked. He couldn't imagine having to fight off the universe for all eternity.

"It will be destroyed when the universe ends, of course," Time answered. The god of creation didn't know what to do. The universe couldn't be destroyed, not even by the combined power of all the Nameless Gods. Chaos had already caused destruction through *disease*; who knows what other evil it could bring. "Commotus," Time spoke again, "It is not in your best interest to consider Chaos your enemy. Declaring war on the universe will end well for no one."

"How can I view something like this as positive?"

Commotus growled.

"You don't – Chaos is neither a positive nor negative force, it simply *is*. It does not work for the benefit of you and your creatures, and it does not work to destroy them. To quote a human who will not be born for many millions of years, 'if it can happen, it will happen.' That is the law of this universe."

Commotus sighed deeply and lowered his head, once again watching his creatures. Many more were now dying than before, but it seemed that just as quickly, more were being born. If he couldn't fight the universe, it seemed that he had no choice but accept it, if not join it.

"Very well," he said. "I will do my best to exist alongside Chaos."

Time did not reply.

Thus was the creation of disease.

Rise of the Maucav

It was a thousand years before anything particularly interesting happened. Not to say that watching creatures live their lives was *boring*, per se, but it was almost like Commotus was becoming immune to the feeling of fascination that came with watching creatures live and die again and again. So it was with great relief that he was summoned from watching the rock, which the humans had renamed Earth, and moved to a place so far on the other side of the not-void that he actually had to turn around and swim to reach it. At first the particular patch of space he was looking at appeared to be empty, but a voice that seemed to flow around him caught his attention.

"Commotus, I have been waiting for you."

"Have you?" Commotus could not find the source of the voice, and so gave up trying to locate it.

"Of course! Ever since my creation, I have been waiting for you to bring me to the rock."

"Have you?"

"My twin sisters and I, yes."

"What are you called?" Commotus asked.

"My name is *Whoosh* and my sisters' names are Lux and Sonus."

"You are the spirits that came with air, and light, and sound, correct?"

"The very same," *Whoosh* replied.

"That was before time! Are there more of you? There should be a spirit of time as well!"

"I haven't seen or heard the spirit of time, if there is one," *Whoosh* said.

"Where are they? Why did none of you ever come to see me? I've been interacting with the spirits of fire, water, and green leafy things since their creation."

"It's against the rules to go to the rock uninvited."

"Said who?"

"Said the Maucav."

Commotus paused for a moment. This spirit was speaking of many things Commotus did not know about. As the god of creation, he felt as if he should know about, well everything. After all, it was he who had turned on the light and invented the not-void. This Maucav must be pretty powerful. Coming to the conclusion that it was not in his best interest to ask about a potential threat he should already know about, Commotus focused his attentions on his unanswered question. "Where is Sonus? And Lux, for that matter?"

"The Maucav have sent Lux on a mission on the rock. Sonus doesn't think the Maucav are telling the truth about the mission, so she chased after Lux to try and stop her."

"When was this?"

"The Maucav communicated their plan to us while you were unable to see them," *Whoosh* explained. Commotus thought briefly of his time stuck in Chaos and shuddered. If there was any time when he would have been unable to see them, it would have been then.

"What is their plan?" Commotus asked, curious.

"They want to destroy your rock and get rid of everything that's been created here," *Whoosh* said. "I think we should stop them now. They're probably already halfway to earth, and I'm pretty sure that Lux is faster than Sonus."

"What if we confront this Maucav first? Will it pull off the attack?" Commotus had an eye turned toward earth, and several more scanning the ever-growing expanse of the not-void.

"I don't think so. I'm pretty sure they've been having the same argument since the beginning of time; they won't just change their minds."

"Wait, this Maucav is a group?" Commotus asked with a growing sense of dread. There was only one group of beings which he had not created. "Are you saying that the Nameless Gods are trying to reclaim the not-void?"

"They're not nameless anymore," *Whoosh* said. "Commotus, we really need to get to the rock before Lux!" Commotus heard a muffled *boom* coming from behind him, and saw a brightness envelop the earth, making it glow as bright as the star it circled. With one enormous movement, Commotus turned himself around and found himself staring at a large battle between the spirits of light and sound. The shockwaves of Sonus as she landed cleared away the wall of light, and Commotus watched as hundreds of his creatures were blasted around, fearful and unable to understand what was happening around them.

"Can't you stop them? You're all powerful, aren't you?" *Whoosh* looked worriedly between earth and its creator.

"I am unable to destroy," Commotus said in reply. The emotions of the creatures were indistinguishable from his.

"So does that mean everyone is going to be destroyed?"

Commotus hesitated for a moment, and for a brief moment caught a glimpse of the other spirits, who were searching the skies, looking for – looking for him! "Infearno!"

The fire spirit focused on him. "Yeah, what is it?" He shouted.

"Do you think you could stop them?"

Infearno watched Lux and Sonus as they tumbled across the sky. "Of course!" With that, he took to the skies, lashing out at both of the dueling spirits. One of his wild blows nailed Lux right in her center, and she dropped to the ground.

"My sister!" *Whoosh* wailed, and within a second he had flown to Lux's side. "How dare you!" He howled at Infearno, who looked like he was considering sinking through the ground. Instead, he grinned cheekily.

"I bet you're just as easy to take down," he said.

With a wordless shriek, *Whoosh* flew at the fire spirit,

who allowed himself to be taken into the skies. In a whirlwind of fury, *Whoosh* tried to smother Infearno, but everything he did only made the fire spirit grow bigger. When he had overtaken a large portion of *Whoosh*'s shapeless form, he freed himself from his grasp and launched himself into the air.

As he fell, Sonus tried to take advantage of the situation and finish off Lux, but was prohibited by William, who up until that point had been silent, only moving to avoid obstacles as they presented themselves.

"Don't you think it's odd that the Maucav only targeted the earth, even though there are many other things they could go after?"

"Hey, don't lecture me, I'm just trying to stop Lux from destroying everything."

"To do so, you would have to destroy her," William replied.

"If that's what it takes, that's what it takes," Sonus said, making a move toward Lux's form.

"Please, consider what I am saying. The Maucav want the not-void to return to its original state. They need to get rid of the things which prevent it from doing so."

"Things like this rock!"

"Things like light, and sound, and air."

Commotus felt a small alarm go off in his head. If William was right, then that meant the Nameless Gods were much smarter than he had originally realized. Smart enough to stop their fighting and join together to fight against him. If they had brainwashed the spirit of light, and tricked Sonus to fight against her, it could have led the spirits to destroy each other. In doing so, it was possible that Lux and Sonus would be removed from existence, plunging everyone back into the void.

Commotus opened his mouth to bring the plot to light: "Wait-"

"THIS WORLD IS MINE!" Infearno screamed. Everyone turned to look at him as his fire raced through grass and trees, spreading around the world in the blink of an eye. The few surviving humans stared at him fearfully. Something about him was very familiar, but they were unable to recall just what it was.

"I AM INFEARNO, GOD OF FIRE, AND ALL WHO SEE ME SHALL BOW BEFORE ME!" The humans jerkily did as they were told, and Commotus could feel their fear.

"Are you serious? Right now, Infearno?" The God of Everything Living and Beautiful and Stuff began walking towards him, her body frail and rather burnt looking.

"I saw an opportunity, and I took it! Nothing wrong with that," Infearno replied, not looking away from his new subjects.

"You are no god, just a bad tempered spirit!"

"MY TEMPER IS WONDERFUL, THANK YOU." The temperature of the surrounding area increased uncomfortably with his words.

"Well, since you're about to destroy me, do you think maybe you could keep it in check?"

"DESTROY Y-" Infearno looked at the God of Everything Living and Beautiful and Stuff, seeing for the first time her frail state. The temperature lowered slightly, and Commotus saw the humans who were on their knees peeking up at the fire spirit. "Did I do that?"

"Yeah, well. I *am* what you are burning up. That hasn't changed since last time you tried to take over the world."

"I see," he replied. "Is there any way to save you?"

"I don't think so," she said.

"In that case," Infearno began. Commotus, not willing to take the chance of Infearno proceeding with his takeover, signaled to *Whoosh* to put his plan in motion.

Creating a strong funnel, he lifted Lux and Sonus into the clouds. The two resumed what appeared to be a fight to the death, and Infearno stopped actively spreading his fire to watch. Meanwhile, William lifted herself into the air above the two earth spirits, spread herself into a big sheet, and dropped all at once, drenching the planet and extinguishing Infearno's power.

GELBS slowly regrew into her full, lush form, and promptly began ignoring Infearno, who appeared to be trying to apologize without actually saying "I'm sorry."

"Commotus, what should we do now?" *Whoosh* asked.

"Rebuild the rock, and make sure that none of the creatures' spirits were damaged by Infearno or the others."

"But what about the Maucav? Won't they be a danger?"

"I don't think so. I'm not sure if you realize this, but they are smaller than dust to me. The only real threat was the destruction of beautiful spirits, and that has been avoided."

"What about me? Where can I go?"

"Well, I assumed you would be staying here, on the rock."

"The rock is forbidden-"

"I never said anything was forbidden. Even Infearno is allowed to do as he pleases," Commotus said. "Mostly."

"Really? And my sisters too?"

"Everyone. If one of the Nameless Gods came to me, and honestly just wished to observe and exist, I would accept it, too."

"You're amazing," *Whoosh* breathed.

"No, I'm just me," Commotus replied, turning to face the earth, feeling something similar to the way a person does at the end of an old fashioned romance movie where a "just married" sign can be seen on the back of a car, or a princess and her knight in shining armor ride off into the sunset.

After three more failed attempts at apologizing to the God of Everything Living and Beautiful and Stuff, Infearno sank into the ground, but not before starting a small fire that would not go out on a rose that would not die.

Lux *did* successfully apologize for putting Sonus through all the trouble of stopping her, and Sonus successfully reciprocated the apology, admitting that trying to kill her was a bit unwarranted.

William slipped away before anyone could speak to

her, disappearing into the flow of the ocean. Commotus found the spirit of water to be the most interesting out of the six he had met so far. She never started any bad business, was always able to quell Infearno, and had no problem interacting with anyone.

Commotus was startled out of his musings by an altercation between Lux and Sonus. It appears they both wished to reside in the clouds, and didn't believe the space was big enough for the both of them. His first instinct was to kick them both out, because the clouds were all he had left of his original creatures, but after having seen their impressive – and rather destructive – fights before, he decided that maybe leaving them there wouldn't be so bad after all.

Thus was the creation of thunder and lightning.

Willow Shipperley

The War of the Spirits

There were many benefits in having everyone speak the same language. Warnings of danger could be communicated faster, for one. It also helped in lessening confusion when transferring messages from group to group, with the exception of one fiasco in which a fox was included in a game of telephone and took the chance to spread panic amongst rabbits with the message "I'm going to feast tomorrow." It was especially helpful if one creature called a meeting of all other creatures, which one human had just done.

"Attention all creatures, this meeting has been called because there is something unnatural occurring on our earth." Adam's voice rang out in the clearing, reaching to the water's edge, and the forest, and the air. She stood at the base of an active volcano, which steadily breathed out sulfuric smoke and ash, and all of the creatures of the rock were gathered as closely around her as they could be. Fish and leviathan both rested in the shallows of pools and in the crests of waves as they crashed to shore; land animals crowded in – shortest in the front, tallest in the back – as close as they could to Adam; birds glided overhead and circled around the smoke.

"Around us have come these beings, beings which are unlike us. They do not have flesh, and they cause massive destruction whenever they pass by." The other Humans and creatures nodded at her statements. It was true, just last week two new beings had come and had a massive battle in the sky, which had blinded and deafened many, and killed more. "As such, there is only one thing we can do: we must drive them all out!"

All of the creatures, from the wolves, to the giraffes, to the fish, to the humans, cheered loudly, and all of their voices sounded the same. Cries of "So true!" came from the elephants, and the starfish gave an energetic "Yeah!"

After waiting for the cheers to die down, Adam continued. "Unfortunately, we are not strong enough to fight these ethereal beings on our own." Discouraged moans swelled from her massive audience. "But there is a way we can still win this." Throwing up her arms, Adam smiled toothily. "There is one who has helped us before, one who has always fought against the others. Therefore, I propose that we enlist the help of-" Adam was suddenly silenced, along with the growing protests of the other creatures, by a deep rumbling coming from deep within the earth.

A great burst of lava sprouted forth from the volcano, scorching the birds who had been too close. Large, flickering hands gripped the lip of the volcano, and out came the super-heated form of the fire spirit.

"I am Infearno, and you shall cower before me!" The creatures could feel the vibrations of his voice in the same way people at concerts feel the bass – in their bones, and in the air filling their lungs. Immediately, Adam fell to her knees, and the rest of the human race copied the motion. Some of the other creatures followed suit, the lions and bears being among them. The vast majority, however, simply stood hesitantly, watching as the enormous spirit of fire lifted himself out of the active volcano. The air was beginning to heat up, and Infearno seemed to be growing larger by the minute as Adam pleaded for his help. Ignoring her, he looked to the rest of Commotus' creatures and shouted, "Why are you not cowering? Bow down before me!"

"I'd really rather not," said one whale from its position in the ocean. "You're a big part of the problem we have here, and I don't think following you will benefit me in any way."

"Yes, well, I'll destroy you if you don't!" Infearno said, with a brief glance upwards. He was bluffing, mostly, but he wasn't too sure if Commotus would realize that.

"See, that's exactly the problem. You're so quick to destroy, and we all really don't like that."

"Nobody cares what you like, whale. What is your name, anyway?"

"I am Tim."

"Hello, Tim. If I say please will you bow down?" The air was beginning to cool, but Infearno did not seem to be shrinking.

"No. Not to *you*, at least."

Infearno narrowed his eyes in confusion. "What do you mean, not to me? Who else-" Infearno was cut off as

William rose from the ocean in a winding, serpentine form.

"Greetings, Infearno. I see you're at it again," she said, nodding towards the humans, who were still on their hands and knees, cowering.

"I was doing quite well, too, until you showed up," Infearno sniffed, looking away from the water spirit with a pout.

"Are you so sure? It looks like most of the creatures here are still standing."

"Well, Tim here was just about to swear fealty to me, now weren't you?" Infearno looked smugly down at the small whale.

"Well, actually, no, I-"

"See? Practically mine already!"

William sighed and rolled her eyes. "You're an idiot, you know that?"

"Me? An idiot? You have the wrong spirit. I think you meant GELBS, because honestly, who picks a name as stupid as that?"

"Excuse me!" Infearno and William both turned to see the God of Everything Living and Beautiful and Stuff standing at the edge of the forest with her hands on her hips.

"Oh, hello, we were just talking about you!" Infearno said. "Come join us!"

"Join *you*? I'd rather get shot into space than *join you*. And for the record, you're the one who came up with that stupid nickname for me."

"Well it's your fault for making it so long in the first

place. It's unreasonable!"

"Unreasonable!" GELBS squeaked.

"GELBS, Infearno, calm down. We don't need another battle right now, especially not with all of Commotus's creatures here." William moved in between the two spirits to keep them separate. The pair glanced fearfully upwards toward the starry sky, wondering if the god of creation was paying attention to them at the moment.

"Well, when I came out of the volcano I accidentally blasted most of the birds out of the air, and he didn't say anything. Maybe he got bored of us." Infearno had a troubled look on his face, as if he were a young child whose parent had stepped out of the house without promising to be back soon.

"Oh, don't be silly. He probably just doesn't want to get involved with the creatures, since they can't remember him, and all," said GELBS with a shrug.

Off in the distance, one human was no longer cowering with his face to the ground. Instead, he was looking up at the starry sky with a small frown on his face. "Come back soon," he whispered. "I think something big is going to happen."

"Simon," another human hissed from the ground. "Get back down before Infearno sees you, or you'll be nothing but a pile of ash!"

Simon looked down at the human, then back up to the sky, which was now covered in dark clouds which had most definitely not been there the last time he'd checked. Slowly, he lowered himself back to the ground, concentrating on listening to the spirits.

"Look, here come Lux and Sonus," William said, gesturing to the dark clouds.

"Oh, what are they doing here?" GELBS asked, looking pleasantly surprised.

"I brought them here," said *Whoosh* as he materialized in front of them.

"*Whoosh*! I haven't seen you for a while! What brings you here?" GELBS asked.

"I heard that someone was going to try and work with Commotus's creatures to take the rest of us down," he said with a frown.

"Is that so?" Infearno asked with a grin. "Can't imagine who that could be."

William sighed. "Look, Infearno, we all know-"

"I did hear that whoever it was is *extremely* good looking, by the way. Hot, even," Infearno said.

"There is no way I am letting you, or anyone else take over the planet and gain control over all of the creatures," *Whoosh* said.

"Try and stop me," Infearno sneered. Moving to join his cowering subjects, Infearno pulled molten lava from the core of the earth, and quickly sealed himself and his creatures in a rock bubble.

GELBS gasped, then turned to the remaining creatures. "Do you want him to rule over everything?"

"Of course not!" came the general reply.

"Then join me, and we will fight him into submission!"

"Yeah!" a portion of the creatures shouted. Most of

them still looked a bit unsure.

A mighty spout of water erupted from the ocean, and the spirits and creatures both turned to see Tim the whale wiggling angrily. "But what about us? I don't want to fight and I bet a lot of the other fishes don't either." Small splashes of agreement from the other fish confirmed his statement.

"Then you can die, for all I care." The God of Everything Living and Beautiful and Stuff turned and stormed into the forests, leaving a stunned *Whoosh* and a silent William.

"That's a bit odd for her," Lux commented from above.

"I think she's upset at Infearno right now, actually. He did insult her name."

"I see," Lux replied.

Tim the whale rolled onto his back in the water with a distressed moan, before righting himself. "Oh, William, I don't want to die."

"You don't have to," William replied.

"But everyone around me is fighting. I'll get killed in the crossfire," he blubbered.

William sighed, and felt sadness solidify in her chest and drop icily into her stomach. As much as she wanted to remain neutral, and just let life run its course, she had an obligation to those creatures which inhabited the waters she was born from. "Water always takes the path of least resistance, and it appears that to do so, I must fight this battle."

"Then I will be on your team!" Tim the whale said.

The voices of other sea creatures echoed his approval.

"I thought you were always supposed to be a neutral party," Sonus shouted from above.

"I am neutral. I will not side with any other spirit. If anything, I am on the side of balance."

"Well, I am on the side of turmoil. I think I want control of everything," Sonus growled.

"Wait, no!" Lux gasped, but Sonus was already gathering the support of different creatures.

Whoosh and Lux both looked around uncertainly, and slowly the remaining creatures aligned themselves with either of the two spirits.

William watched sadly as Sonus whirled away with her creatures. This hadn't exactly been a part of her plan to stop Infearno from baking the world, but it seemed inevitable that the spirits would get sucked into this. She stood for a few moments, searching unsuccessfully for a break in the clouds that would allow her to see Commotus, before diving deep into the waters of the ocean with her pledged creatures.

Far away, nearly on the other side of the universe, Commotus was looking. He wasn't sure what he was looking *for*, exactly, but a hollowness inside of him was aching to be filled by... something. The vagueness of the situation frustrated him, but he couldn't shake the feeling. He'd been floating around the not-void for a while, careful to avoid any patches of darkness that made him feel cold and uneasy. He'd stopped a few times to make things for small rocks. He was careful not to make anything that would result in a spirit, because so far over here he wasn't sure if he'd be able to keep an eye on them. None of the Maucav attempted to stop him from creating. A few even proclaimed that *they* had made the beings, which further proved that they were better than everyone else, so *there*. Commotus allowed them to keep their delusions, if it would stop them from destroying that which was now living. There was one creation that Commotus bonded with enough to want to take back with him when he returned to earth. It had a cylindrical brown center, with brown limbs sprouting from it, and a thin green coating of needle-like hairs. It named itself the "Evergreen."

Giving up on his search for Something for the moment, Commotus turned and began his trip back through the not-void, being careful not to expose the Evergreen to the suffocating lack of everything. As he approached his favorite rock – earth, as it was known by its inhabitants – he noticed that it appeared to be completely covered in dark clouds. If he had a heart, it would have skipped a beat at that moment. The appearance was thicker than the black fog he'd come to know, but for a second, all Commotus could see was Chaos.

"Hello, Sonus? Lux? What are you doing?" he called down to the planet.

There was a few seconds of silence, and then Lux briefly surfaced to face Commotus. "There's a war. Sound is trying to use the cloud cover to control the air, but *Whoosh* keeps blowing them away."

"What?" Commotus gasped.

"Well, you know, *Whoosh* can sort of blow things around, it's kind of what he does."

"No, no, no. There's a *war*?"

"Oh, yeah. That started a while ago."

"*Why* exactly is there a war?"

"Because the creatures didn't like us spirits fighting all the time, so they got together to try and figure out a plan to drive us out."

"And as a result, now the spirits are fighting?"

Lux paused. "Well, if you want to put like that, yeah."

Commotus was at a loss for what to do. How could things have disintegrated so quickly into fights? He'd only been gone for a few decades. Now he felt bad for bringing Evergreen over; there was no way he could put it down amidst all of the fighting.

"What sparked the spirits' fighting? If it was the creatures which started it, the spirits should know better than to endanger them."

"Well, the human known as Adam was rallying the creatures, and said that there was one spirit who could help them. One who always fought against the other spirits."

Commotus groaned. "It was Infearno, wasn't it?"

Lux simply nodded. Commotus sighed, and manually cleared clouds away to assess the situation himself. A stomach-twisting feeling of uneasiness rippled through him, and he was unsurprised to note the black fog twisting around the feet of his creatures and the spirits. There was no way an entire *war* could have broken out without the presence of Chaos.

Unaware of the fog, Infearno was molding molten lava into blockades and enormous shields to protect the humans and other creatures, and GELBS was knocking them down just as fast. William and *Whoosh* were locked in a winding battle through the air and underwater, and their creatures were clashing in a similar way. Sonus boomed above, doing her best to deafen her opponents, and Lux danced nervously back and forth near Commotus.

"*Runter!*" Infearno roared, and Commotus watched as all of the creatures under his command dropped to the ground. He blasted a large flame in a circle above their heads, scorching the green leafy territory and causing the God of Everything Living and Beautiful and Stuff to scream.

Commotus turned to Lux. "What did Infearno just tell them? That's not a word in our language."

"The spirits have started making code words, so they can be more secretive about their battle strategies."

"*Angriff!*" he shouted, pointing toward the opposition. The humans and other creatures leaped up and charged forward, clashing with the creatures under GLEBS's command.

"*¡Defenderse!*" she cried.

"That one sounded different!" Commotus exclaimed. Although the terror of his creatures was pounding through his veins, he couldn't help but feel just a small sliver of delight. They had created something all by themselves!

"Défendez-vous!" Whoosh cried, and Commotus turned to see William and her creatures flowing forward to overcome *Whoosh*'s.

"They're different, but they're the same," Commotus marvelled.

"勝つ! *Katsu!*" William called as encouragement.

"This is amazing."

"Is it? I mean, they are fighting, and lots of the creatures are dying," Lux said.

Commotus frowned. "I suppose you're right. This isn't good."

"They're so caught up in the fight, they don't even know you're here."

"True." Commotus wasn't really listening to Lux anymore, her comment had reminded him of the toll this was taking. Searching the mobs of creatures, Commotus tried desperately to locate Simon, the beautiful soul that remembered him. He was standing off to the edge of battle, close to the cover of the trees.

"Simon," he whispered.

The man looked around, startled and jumpy. "Who's there?"

"It is I, Commotus, god of creation."

"Commotus! You're here!" Simon brightened considerably, searching the skies to find the god.

"Yes, I am here. I need you to take a message to the others."

Simon glanced towards the raging battle that encompassed the land. "You want me to go in there?"

The hesitation and fear emanating from the human

was threatening to impede the clarity of Commotus's mind. "I can't promise your safety, Simon. I can, however, make sure your spirit remains undamaged."

"My spirit?"

"The immortal piece inside of you that is what you are."

"Okay," Simon said.

"Okay, you understand, or okay, you'll go?" Commotus's mind was beginning to get fuzzy from the amount of terror and anger flowing through the creatures.

"Okay, I'll go. I do not understand you or your ways, but I trust you."

"Really? Oh, I mean – of course. I need you to go into the fray, and demand that everyone stop fighting."

"Do you think they'll listen?" Simon asked, glancing doubtfully at the fray.

"The spirits will listen. The creatures will follow their lead," Commotus said confidently.

"Okay," Simon said, and without looking back he walked straight for the mob of creatures and spirits. Commotus had to force himself not to call the human back to him out of fear.

Glancing toward Evergreen, he said, "It's not always like this, you know. When this all dies down I'll put you into the forest, so you can blend in." The Evergreen rustled in reply.

"Humans! Fellow creatures! I carry a message!" Simon was in the middle of the battlefield, with his arms raised above his head. The creatures around him paid no attention to his words. "We must stop this fight at once!"

Infearno, who was watching the battle with glee, noticed the odd human who was not following his commands. "You there," he shouted. "What are you doing?"

"I carry a message," Simon replied.

"A message? From who, GELBS?"

"No, from Commotus."

The smile dropped off of Infearno's face. "What does he want?"

"A cease-fire."

Infearno glanced upwards at the mostly cloudy sky. "Did he say what he would do if we didn't listen?"

"Well, he just said that you *would* listen," Simon replied.

"How do you even know who Commotus is?"

"Well, I'm not sure, exactly, because I've never really seen him before, but-"

"You're lying. You just overheard us talking about him. He isn't here, and this is my world now." Simon stared helplessly up at the fire spirit as he pointed back towards the battle. "*Gehen jetzt kämpfen!*"

Simon simply wandered back to the edge of the forest. "Commotus, they didn't listen to me."

Commotus sighed. "I know, Simon. It looks like I'm going to have to resort to desperate measures."

"What are you going to do?"

"I'm going to break the land apart, and physically keep them away from each other."

"You can do that?" Simon breathed, looking towards the sky in wonder.

"Of course I can. I made the land you stand on, the air you breathe, and the food you eat. I can do whatever I need to keep things in balance."

"You're amazing."

"No, I'm just the god of creation. I need you to go back, this time with a new message."

"Of course, what is it?"

"Tell Infearno that I will not allow him to take over the world. Demand that all spirits cease fire and return to their homes, or they will be forced apart by me."

"Yes, of course. But, why don't you just tell them yourself?"

"I can't let the other creatures hear me. They cannot handle knowing me the way you do. You somehow retained your memory when I removed myself from all the creatures' minds, which allows you to be my messenger."

Simon frowned. "Well, okay."

"Good luck," Commotus said, and with that Simon walked back over to Infearno, who was now approaching fifty feet in height.

"Infearno! I have another message!"

"Back already?" Infearno turned from his latest work of molten rock to face the human.

"Commotus said that he will not allow you or anyone else to take over the world, and he says that if everyone doesn't cease fire and return to their homes, he will force you apart."

"I don't believe you," Infearno said.

"Well, are you willing to suffer the consequences?"

"Commotus is a being of creation. He can't destroy me without destroying everything else as well. I'll take my chances."

"Well, will you at least tell the other spirits, so that they can make their own decisions?"

Infearno sighed. "Fine. All spirits! This human has a 'message' from Commotus!" The spirits immediately stopped fighting, although the creatures continued. "Well?" Infearno turned to look down at Simon.

"Ah, well, he told me that you guys all need to stop, or he'll, um, force you apart."

GELBS started laughing. "How eloquent! You don't even know who you're talking about, human."

"Yes I do! Commotus is the god of creation, and he talks to me."

"Right. Well, I don't know if I believe you."

"I sure don't! I'm going to keep fighting until I control the whole world!" Infearno had a large smile on his face.

"I can't just sit back and *let* him take over, so I'm going to keep fighting too," GELBS said. William, Lux and Sonus nodded in agreement.

"Well, okay, then," Simon said, with a nervous glance up at the sky.

"*Criaturas, atacan ahora!*" shouted the God of Everything Living and Beautiful and Stuff, reverting back to her code language.

"Yeah, attack!" chorused Lux and Sonus.

The creatures and spirits clashed again, harder and more energetically than before. It lasted for about half a minute before a great, deep rumbling seemed to take over, coming from the ground.

"What is that?" GELBS shrieked.

"It is Commotus. He is separating you," Simon said.

"No!" William gasped.

"That's not fair!" Infearno howled.

"It's completely fair," Simon said. "I did warn you. Twice."

By now the creatures had stopped fighting completely, and were now crying out in terror, still using the code languages the spirits had made up for them.

Commotus came down to the earth as close as he dared, and whispered to Simon, "Repeat after me."

"Spirits of the rock, I speak to you now directly," Simon shouted. They all turned, cowering, towards the human. "I will not allow one being to rule my rock. I have created you, and I have allowed you to live and prosper here, even after you destroyed my dinosaurs, and killed many of my new creatures. This is unacceptable. I cannot destroy you, but you need to be punished. Therefore, I shall now split the surface of the rock into pieces. Each of you shall inhabit a piece, and none of you will try to become a ruler. Am I understood?"

"Yes, Commotus," the group of spirits mumbled, looking for all the world like a group of naughty children who had just been scolded by their mother.

"Good." With that, Commotus backed away from the rock and, in a burst of concentration that – nearly – rivaled the creation of time, separated the land on the rock into separate masses, without killing anybody.

Infearno, the humans, and other loud creatures were grouped on one mass, the God of Everything Living and Beautiful and Stuff inhabited a heavily forested area with a variety of creatures, and William was confined to the waters in between. Lux and Sonus were separated and given pieces of land, and Commotus finally set down the Evergreen with GELBS, so that it might make friends with the trees. *Whoosh* was given the air, and all the creatures who inhabited it.

The main passtime for Infearno and the other spirits became making up more words for their languages. These words quickly surpassed war terms and attacks, and soon everybody was labelling everything in different secret codes. After many years, during the spirits' banishments, the original language faded from memory, and when the last creature from the war began its journey to the black hole, it was erased forever, except in the minds of the spirits, and Commotus.

Thus was the creation of different languages.

The Ancient Pyramids

Nothing exciting had happened for nearly 200 million years. When Commotus had split the land in order to separate the spirits and punish them for their foolish war, he hadn't expected them to stay isolated from one another for so long. Even Lux and Sonus, who had free reign over the entire planet through the clouds along with their land masses, had not spoken to the Spirits on land. They barely spoke to each other, either, as if they were nervous they would be separated if they did. *Whoosh* had been staying close to the ground, sweeping over the plant life again and again until only the toughest low lying shrubs remained. It was almost like they were *sulking*.

Which, as a matter of fact, is *exactly* what they were doing. For the first hundred thousand years, all of the spirits had rampaged, angrily destroying the land they'd been banished to and the people with them, but afterwards they'd withdrawn, isolating themselves the way children sometimes do when they think they've been bad. Commotus watched them sadly from beside a distant planet, where he was currently trying to figure out how he could make it rain sideways. Part of him wanted to reach out and hold them all to him, so they could feel the searing ferocity with which he loved them, but another part of him wanted to wait the whole thing out. It could give him insight into how they worked, he reasoned. So he waited, and watched, and felt the stinging hurt of being ignored and forgotten as it rose from the spirits.

Many times, he found himself unknowingly swimming through the not-void in order to be closer to his favorite planet, but he always pulled himself back in time. He thought that if he waited just a little bit longer, something would change in the emotions, and he would be able to swoop in. Maybe they would even apologize for their actions. But as time ticked by, and Commotus realized it had been 200 million years since he had last spoken to the spirits, he knew he had to go to them. At first, he wasn't sure how to approach them. After all, the last time they'd spoken was through a human, and he was banishing them. After a futile search for Simon, Commotus admitted that even if he had found his Listener, he couldn't just have a human show up and start talking. He was going to have to appear as himself.

As he made his way into a proper position to face the spirits, he took a deep breath and tried to gather his thoughts. This was his chance to reintroduce himself – what should he say? To gain an understanding of how he should reenter the lives of the spirits, Commotus focused his attentions on their emotions only, and let himself fully experience what it was *they* were feeling. Instead of the anger and bitterness he had been sure they were full of, he felt a longing constrict his insides. Curling in on himself, Commotus felt his perception that he was separate from them slip away. He lost his feelings of omnipotence, and for an undeterminable length of time existed only in the anguish of the spirits. His spirits.

His spirits! Commotus struggled to withdraw himself from the emotions, pushing back the feelings of his creations until he was certain his mind was separate from theirs. In the absence of their longing, Commotus felt hollow. He could still feel a longing, but this was not *their* longing. It was a small echo, which had gone unnoticed for the most part. Until now, that is, for in the sudden absence of such overwhelming emotion, all of the little pieces of himself that he hadn't noticed were now glaringly visible.

When he opened his mouth to speak, he panicked, suddenly doubting the eloquent apology-statements, and instead blurted out something akin to, "Hey guys, what's up?"

The spirits, who had been going about their days as usual, were startled to hear a voice they'd nearly forgotten, in a language that hadn't been spoken since the War, 200 million years ago.

"Commotus, is that you?" William asked, surfacing from the depths of an ocean which would remain unexplored by humans for many thousands of years.

The god of creation was so busy replaying what he'd said over and over again in his head that he almost didn't hear the water spirit. As it was, he managed to let out a sigh of "yeah, it's me," before hesitantly looking back down at the earth.

"You're back!" Infearno shouted joyfully. "I've missed you very much!"

"I've missed you too, Infearno," Commotus said hesitantly. The open display of happiness wasn't what he was expecting after being gone for so long. He'd been looking for a more "oh no, the evil creator is back to lecture me and foil my plans at world domination" sort of response, but he supposed that he was oversimplifying the fire spirit. If he'd learned anything from his – admittedly limited – interactions with Infearno, it was that he was passionate in everything he did, no matter if it was a takeover, or a greeting.

GELBS appeared to hang back, and avoided looking directly at him. He was about to speak to her directly, but his attention was diverted by the sudden appearance of Lux, Sonus, and *Whoosh*.

"Sorry we're a bit late, we almost didn't hear you over the storm we were brewing over a massive rainforest," Sonus explained.

"It's fine, really," Commotus said. He was definitely not as attached to these three spirits, although they had been spawned before Infearno, William, and the God of Everything Living and Beautiful and Stuff. It was nice that they came, though. Not a second passed after that thought crossed his mind before a wave of guilt splashed through him. He couldn't pick *favorites*! Not only was that massively unfair, but it was clear from their excited looks and admiring glances that they loved him very much. Commotus smiled wider at the three spirits and added, "I'm just glad you could make it."

Trying not to look too dismissive of them, he turned his attention to GELBS, who was pointedly ignoring him. "Hey, GELBS? What's wrong?"

She did not reply, but looked pointedly toward the horizon, directly below her creator.

Commotus sighed. He supposed he should be grateful that only one of the six appeared to be unhappy with him, when he'd expected all of them to be a bit touchy, but it was still disappointing. "I did not expect the God of Everything Living and Beautiful and Stuff to come bounding joyfully to see me, but I do hope you can at least talk to me," he said.

She turned her gaze up to the starry sky that was Commotus. "I'm not mad," she said with a sniff, "I just think there's a bit of explaining to do."

Commotus nodded. "I didn't mean to be away so long, and I am sorry that your punishment became such a big deal. I was panicked, and angry, and I needed to separate you before you destroyed all of my creatures." After a pause, he added, "And the world."

"Well, it wasn't my fault! It was Infearno's fault. He always goes too far," she replied.

"Hey," Infearno cried, with a wounded look.

"Please, now is not the time to fight," Commotus said, trying his best to stop the oncoming argument. The two spirits looked at the god of creation sullenly.

"Is there a specific reason you came back?" William asked. Commotus silently thanked her for redirecting the other spirits' collective attention.

"I came back to apologize. I never meant for this to

go on so long."

"Well, you've apologized, so now can you fix the land and leave us alone?" GELBS asked.

"Actually, I don't think so. About either of the things you asked."

"What do you mean?" asked *Whoosh*.

"The land has been split, and William has filled the spaces in between. She has been eating away at the jagged edges of the rock, and now they won't fit back together just right. Also, I don't plan on leaving again very soon. I want to stay here and interact with you."

The God of Everything Living and Beautiful and Stuff rolled her eyes, but did not speak.

"So, what will happen now?" Lux and Sonus asked together.

"I suppose it will be like it was before the War. My creatures still can't know about me, though. It would destroy them."

"I barely remember what it was like back then," Infearno said.

"What happens if you have to leave again, and something bad happens while you're gone?" GELBS spoke up.

Commotus frowned down at the spirits. "I don't know why I *would* have to leave."

"I bet you didn't know you *would* have to leave us alone for 200 million years, either," she countered.

"I guess we should set up a signal of some sort."

"Can it be loud and flashy?" Lux and Sonus asked.

"Can it be something that can get around every

obstacle?" William asked.

"Can it be powerful and hot?" Infearno asked excitedly.

"Can it be swift and agile?' asked *Whoosh*.

"Can it be something that grows and adapts?" asked GELBS softly.

"I can try my best," Commotus said, stunned by their rapid-fire questions.

As it turned out, most of the requests were squeezed in, one way or another. The structure had a square base that tapered as it went up until the four triangular sides met together in one point at the top. It was made of white stone, and the flashiness was added when the tip was covered in gold, but the rest of the requests came in the actual alert Commotus would receive. It would come in a form of concentrated electricity, powered when all of the spirits came together and touched the four sides of the shape. The electricity would shoot up to the sky and connect with the stars making up Commotus's pelt.

After a bit of discussion, it was decided that there should be more of these structures, on the other land masses. Each spirit should be able to send power through a different structure, they reasoned, so that no one would be struggling to get to where they needed to be, if the time ever arose. From the suggestion of GELBS, Commotus added a failsafe so that if one of the spirits was unable to reach one of the structures, the others would still be able to send the signal.

When it was done, the spirits dispersed, until only GELBS remained. "Commotus?" she asked softly.

The god of creation turned to her small form, and he felt his stomach flutter nervously. "What is it, earth spirit?"

"Thank you for coming back," she mumbled, and before Commotus could reply, she was on her way back to her own land.

Thus was the creation of the pyramids.

The Colors of the Sky

The creatures of the rock were not oblivious to the changes they saw in the spirits. Infearno was even more joyful than usual. In fact, he was so happy that his heat evaporated all the water on his piece of land, and had to be replenished by William. The fish of the sea had caught their water spirit *singing* a few days ago. All of the plants in the forests and swamps were in full bloom, and GELBS danced around with the creatures on her land. *Whoosh* was whipping around, leaving a sweet smell wherever he went, and Lux and Sonus were both romping around in the clouds like there was no tomorrow.

However, none of the spirits would answer the creatures when they asked what had happened, leaving only a vague, "the weather is nice," or a wistful, "I just like this time of year."

They were stuck at a bit of a stalemate here: if they didn't know what caused the happy mood, they wouldn't be able to prevent things from changing for the worse, and if they kept asking, they might annoy the spirits, which would then end the happy mood they were all in.

It wasn't long before a fox noticed that GELBS always seemed to be looking up at the sky nowadays. This information was quickly passed along, and confirmed with the other five spirits as well. The creatures decided that the spirits' sudden happiness was at least partially related to *something in the sky*. What it was, they didn't know, but they were determined to find out.

Many birds were sent on missions up above the clouds to examine the sky. It didn't appear to be any different, but something had to have changed. It was just as starry as they could remember. Maybe the constellations had changed? With this apparent block stopping their investigation in their tracks, the creatures turned to the spirits, carefully asking questions about the sky, and watching their expression changes carefully as they listened to the answers

"What's your favorite part of the sky?" an eel asked William one morning.

"Oh, I dunno, the stars I guess," she replied with a large smile.

The other creatures turned up similar results. The stars, the darkness, the sun, the stars, the stars, the sun. It was not unanimous.

"Maybe you were wrong," one rabbit hesitantly suggested to the fox.

"There's got to be a connection, though!" He paced back and forth in front of the motley crew of animals in front of him. "We just have to figure out what it is."

Commotus had been watching *Whoosh* for a while now as he swooped and spun through the air above the land and water. "Watch me do this!" he shouted happily as he turned himself into a tight funnel and corkscrewed

The Colors of the Sky

through the air. Commotus laughed at his childlike antics and was about to ask him to do it again when the congregation of creatures led by the fox caught his attention.

"Hold on, *Whoosh*, I want to look at this," he said, turning his attention to the group without waiting for an answer.

"If only we could see what they are thinking when they look up at the sky," a lion mused.

"I still think it was a weak connection to begin with," stated the rabbit. "After all, maybe they're just happy! We all get happy for no reason sometimes."

"But all of them got happy at the same time," the fox said. "I'm sure there's a connection. I mean, have you ever seen GELBS this happy before?" The rabbit shook her head. "Well, then there's no way to prove that it isn't the sky, unless we take it away.

"There's no way we could do that," the lion grumbled, looking upwards past the clouds. "We can't just do nothing, though. The only thing worse than not knowing what made the spirits happy, is not knowing how to fix it when they get sad."

The rabbit and fox both nodded. "We'll have to keep pressing them for information, then. Hopefully one of them will slip up."

With that, the creatures dispersed. Commotus stared at where they'd been, stomach churning uneasily. He couldn't let them figure out what was really going on. Maybe if he left for a while, the creatures would see them looking sadly at the sky. Then they wouldn't know *what* to think. Commotus shook his head. He couldn't do that! Besides, the confusion wouldn't last forever. His creatures were very smart. What else could he do?

"Hey, *Whoosh*, can I ask you something?"

"Sure, what is it?" he asked, appearing breathlessly in front of his creator.

"Do you think you could bring a message to the other spirits? Tell them to tone down their excitement, maybe?"

"Yeah, of course!" he agreed happily before rocketing off. A few seconds later he was back. "Uh, why, exactly?"

"The creatures are getting suspicious. I don't want them to figure out that you're happy *I'm* back, because they won't be able to handle knowing me."

"Okay," he said, and quickly disappeared again. Commotus sat back and began thinking about what else he could do to throw the creatures off his trail, but *Whoosh* was back before he could formulate a complete thought.

"William, Lux, and Sonus said okay, Infearno and GELBS wanted to talk to you."

Commotus sighed. He hoped this wouldn't become a big deal. "Follow me," he said to the air spirit, before moving around the planet to find the two spirits.

"Infearno," he called out. A few seconds later, the flaming spirit appeared below him.

"Why do you want us to hide our happiness about you coming back?"

The Colors of the Sky

"Because I can't let the creatures find out what's really going on," Commotus replied.

"It's not secretly because you don't want us to be happy?" GELBS asked as she appeared next to Infearno.

"What? Of course not!" Commotus was shocked. Was her trust in him so fragile? He supposed that it was acceptable, since he'd only been back for a few weeks, and he'd been gone for 200 million years or so.

"Then I don't see why I should pretend not to be happy," GELBS said. "Although, if this conversation keeps on this track, I don't think that'll be a problem."

Commotus's heart sank. It was never going to be easy, was it? "Well, if you can convince the creatures around you that your happiness has nothing to do with the sky, or me, then I think everything will be okay."

"So you want me to *lie* to you creatures, Commotus?" GELBS asked. Infearno's fire began to dim down a bit at the negative turn in conversation, and the air became noticeably cooler.

"You know what? I have a better idea," he said.

"What is it?" Commotus asked, desperate for anything that would improve the situation.

"What if we change the way the sky looks? That way, everyone thinks that we – the Spirits, I mean – were planning this secret surprise for them. That would stop people questioning us about our good moods, and they'll accept it because it's related to the sky!"

"That's actually quite a good idea," GELBS mumbled. Commotus nodded in agreement.

"That just might work. But, how would we change the color of the sky? I *am* the sky." Commotus asked.

"You could create something to be in front of you for part of the time. It could be really pretty: orange and yellow and red!"

"Or green," GELBS said.

"Or blue," William cut in, coming out of the water they were near. "I think this plan could work!"

Rather quickly, since he didn't want to give his creatures any more time to discover him than he had to, Commotus fashioned a sort of cloak to wear. Starting as dark as the not-void by the collar, the colors moved in a gradient to inky blue, purple, red, orange, pink, white, and blue, and then in reverse until it reached black again at the edges. It was decided it would be on during the daytime, when most of the creatures were awake, and at night he would take it off so the spirits could still be comforted by his image.

Afterwards, Commotus found the same group of animals talking.

"I told you," the fox yipped excitedly. "I told you it had something to do with the sky!"

The rabbit frowned, looking up at the vibrant blue covering the sky. "I guess you're right," she said with a frown. "I just feel like something's still missing."

"Oh, don't be such a downer," the lion growled, "You're just upset that the fox was right and you were wrong."

"Maybe," said the rabbit.

The Colors of the Sky

Commotus breathed a sigh of relief, and resumed watching *Whoosh* spin through the air, happily.

Thus was the creation of the colors of the sky.

Willow Shipperley

And Then There Were Dreams

"I don't know how it happened. One minute I was just sitting here, enjoying the sunlight and the beautiful blue of the sky, and then I was *in* the sky. Flying!" The rabbit was sitting haphazardly in the dirt, eyes wide, nose twitching. Her fur was messy and stuck up in tufts.

"How'd you get back down then?" the fox asked.

"Well, I – I don't know. It was like as soon as I realized that I was flying, I was back here on the ground," she answered, kneading the ground with her paws uneasily. "It felt wonderful, but I'm afraid the feeling's already starting to fade."

The fox's tail drooped. "And you're sure you don't know how to do it again?"

"No, I don't think that could happen. I can barely remember it anymore."

"Well that's no fun. You should tell me if it happens again," the fox said before disappearing into the bushes with a flick of his tail.

"R-right," the rabbit replied. With a wary glance up at the sky, she hopped away from the edge of the forest and towards the long-grassed plains that housed her burrow.

The next day, there was a massive panic amongst a flock of sheep, when one woke up bleating of having swum like a fish in the ocean. Of course, this lead to all of the other sheep saying that they, too, had been like fish in the ocean. This was a great cause of concern for them, since sheep generally do not know how to breathe underwater. In fact, they were so unhappy that they began a small stampede, which woke up all of the other creatures that lived near the border of the forest and the plains.

"Help, help!" They bleated. "We've been turned into fish and we don't know how to swim!" A lion was sent out to stop them before they damaged anything, but the sheep did not respond well to that. "A great big lion has come to scoop us out of the water and eat us!" they chorused.

"You know, we could just let them run until they get tired," the fox said to the rabbit, who had been woken up when the hooves of the sheep had nearly broken through the roof of her burrow. "Maybe when they've settled down we can figure out what it is they're talking about."

The rabbit twitched her ears. "I don't think that's a good idea."

"Why not?"

"Well, remember last time they stampeded? It took them ages to realize that the 'monster' chasing them was simply a wolf, and when they told them so, they took off again for another half hour!"

"Well, do you have any idea why they're going around thinking they're fish?"

"No, not really. I mean – never mind," the rabbit said, nose scrunched up.

"Tell me! I'd love to know what you're thinking," the fox said, wrapping his large red tail around his small friend.

"I was sort of thinking that maybe it's related to when I flew yesterday."

"How so? Flying and swimming are not very similar, to my knowledge."

"N-neither of us know how to do the things we know we've done, really, but we've both got the memories. It's odd, but I feel there's some kind of connection." The rabbit hunched close to the ground, kneading the long grass underneath her feet. "It's making me nervous though."

The fox leaned closer to his friend, unsure what to say. "Maybe we should go talk to the other creatures?"

The rabbit twitched her ears again before hopping forward towards the forest. The fox then quickly ran off to go get the lion away from the panicked sheep, collecting other creatures as he went. When he made it to the clearing where GELBS had decided Meetings would be held, the rabbit was already there, asleep by a tree stump.

"Hey, rabbit, wake up," the fox said, nudging her small form with one paw.

"Waah!" came her reply, before she bolted from where she'd been sleeping and ran blindly into the paws of a wolf.

"Rabbit! Are you okay?" the fox asked.

"I-I was flying again! It was wonderful, but so terrifying!" She had the same wide-eyed look she'd had the last time the fox had heard about her flight.

"No you weren't! I was right here, and I woke you up!" the fox had sat down, and had his head tilted to the side in confusion.

"That's impossible! I very clearly remember-" the rabbit trailed off.

"Remember what?" the wolf she'd run into prompted.

"Well, it's a bit fuzzy now, but I could have sworn I was flying before."

"We all saw you sleeping here, so obviously you weren't. Were you lying to me before, too?" The fur on the fox's back was spiked up defensively, but the way his head was drooping betrayed his upset.

"Of course I'm not lying! I'm just as confused as you should be! What about the sheep, then, any idea why they think they're fish?"

"They're liars too," the fox growled, showing his teeth.

The rabbit shrank back into the wolf, who was very unsure of what he should do. Just then, the lion stepped in between the creatures. "That's enough," he growled. "All of us here know that sheep don't have ideas of their own. Someone must have given them the idea before they panicked."

"I bet it was the rabbit. Did you want to get back at

me for being right about the Gods making the sky colorful as a surprise?"

"I was never mad about that, fox. I was just a little unsure that *that* was the reason for GELBS and the other gods being so happy!"

"You didn't deny that it was you who gave them the idea, though-"

"Silence!" the lion roared. "Cease this petty bickering. Someone genuinely scared the sheep enough to make them stampede, and singling out a rabbit with no motive is not going to help anybody."

"I sort of think that *you* are the one who did that to the sheep, fox," the wolf said. "After all, you do love pranks! What's to say that this isn't one of them?"

"I wouldn't do a prank and then bring all of the creatures to a meeting to figure out what's going on! I would just sit on the sidelines and watch you all run yourselves ragged." The fox had his teeth bared, and looked as if he was ready to leap right at the wolf.

Before anyone could speak, however, GELBS appeared in the clearing. "Creatures! What are you doing? Is there a Meeting taking place?"

"Something like that," the lion replied, shifting from paw to paw uneasily.

"Well, what's the meeting about?"

"We came here to talk about why the sheep think they're fish. Rabbit thought that it might have a connection to her memories of flying."

"Memories of flying! That sounds marvelous, rabbit, but how did you achieve such a thing without wings?"

GELBS smiled widely at the rabbit, who was considerably less upset in her presence.

"I don't know exactly, and the memories are a bit odd-"

"Which is because rabbit is a liar!" the fox yelped.

"Are you lying rabbit?" GELBS asked, turning her gentle smile on the small animal.

"No, I don't think so," she replied.

"Well, I believe that rabbit is telling the truth to the best of her ability, fox."

"But she was sleeping! I came over to wake her up, and as soon as she woke up she started talking about how she'd been flying! How can she be flying and asleep at the same time?"

"That is a good question. I am sure there is an answer here, if you only want to look for it. However, this Meeting was called because the sheep think that they are fish?"

"Yes, and they are very upset about it. They haven't stopped their stampede since they woke up this morning!" the lion said. "In fact, they were up before the rest of us, and it was their terrified bleating that woke all of us up."

"I see. Can you all think of anything the two events have in common?" The sun was beginning to set at this point, but GELBS let off a warm green glow that was becoming more visible the darker it got.

"They both have sleeping in common," a deer said.

"That's right. So, something must have happened relating to sleep, which has affected rabbit, the sheep, and the humans."

"Wait, the humans are flying, too?" the fox asked.

"Yes, they appear to think they've flown, burrowed, and swam all across the earth."

"It's too bad none of them speak our language, or maybe we could ask them some questions," the rabbit said softly.

"Wait, there's no way you could have tricked the humans, rabbit. What's going on, then?" the fox asked, his tail flicking nervously.

"Well, fox, that's what we are trying to figure out. Can you think of anything that could connect the humans to the experiences of rabbit and the sheep?" GELBS asked with a smile. The sun had fully set, and the colors of the sky had faded away to reveal the never-ending expanses of stars. GELBS's green glow was now fully visible and it cast strange shadows on the ground from the creatures and the trees.

"Do the humans say they've done these things after they sleep?" fox asked.

"Yes, as a matter of fact, they do. Does anyone have an idea as to why this is?"

"Maybe when we are sleeping, we go to other places where we *can* do those things," the rabbit ventured.

"That's a possibility," GELBS said.

"That doesn't explain why the sheep would go somewhere that scares them so much. They don't have original thoughts, so why would they go anywhere at all?" the deer asked.

"Well, what if something else chooses where they

go?" the wolf suggested.

"That could make sense, but that brings us back to another question," the fox said. "What gave the sheep the idea in the first place?"

GELBS smiled, and her glow became brighter. Miniscule dust motes appeared briefly in the air, shimmering in a way similar to sparks rising above an open fire, before fading out of view again.

"What was that?" the rabbit gasped in wonder. "Can you bring those back?"

"What, the glowing particles?" GELBS asked. When she smiled again, they briefly shimmered into being before fading back into the green light.

The creatures gasped happily. "They look like stars," the fox yipped. With the investigation temporarily forgotten, the creatures pleaded with GELBS to let them see the golden sparks. Not long after, all of the creatures began to slip into the darkness of sleep.

"I'm sorry for turning on you, rabbit," the fox whispered as he fought to keep his eyes open. The rabbit silently made her way over to her red-furred friend and burrowed into his fur, falling asleep almost immediately. The fox looked up at the glowing golden sparks and watched them move slowly through the air in the dark clearing. As sleep began to blur his vision, he noticed that the little specks fit in perfectly with the starry night sky.

When the fox finally allowed himself to settle next to the rabbit and sleep he had barely closed his eyes before he felt himself being lifted into the air. After a momentary panic, during which he tried in vain to run away, the fox realized that he had been suspended in the midst of the beautiful golden sparks. All around him, they floated and swirled lazily through the air in complex patterns that mesmerized him, and filled him with a soft warmth that seemed to settle his heart and calm his mind. Some small part of him remembered a feeling similar to this, from a long time ago – much longer than he'd been alive on the planet. It was the memory of a feeling that, even as an echo, was just as strong as what the little golden sparks were filling him with.

For a second, when he looked up and caught a glimpse of the starry sky above him, the feeling became too much for him to understand. The fox thrashed, trying to find some physical way to displace the strength of the warmth that seemed to be overflowing from him. The golden sparks began to break away from their complex swirling patterns, and soon it seemed that all of the tiny glowing particles had moved to surround him. When they touched him, the fox felt the overwhelming emotion drain away, until all that was left was an echo of content.

GELBS stayed with the creatures until she was sure all of them had fallen asleep, and then she released the glowing particles down onto them. A few of the animals made noises in their sleep, but the fox was the only one to move. The movements lasted only a few minutes, after which, he settled down into a silent sleep.

Looking up to the limitless expanses of the night sky, the God of Everything Living and Beautiful and Stuff whispered, "I have done as you asked, Commotus. These particles seem to be a workable solution – the brain and spiritual activity of every creature has dipped back to normal levels."

"Even the fox?" Commotus asked.

"Yes, even the fox. However, when he did fall asleep, his spirit had a massive spike in color before it calmed down with everyone else's. Do you think he's going to be okay?"

"I saw what you described, GELBS. He will be fine. I need you to go teach Infearno and William how to make those particles now, while all of the creatures are sleeping. *Whoosh* will take you over to Infearno now."

"Of course, Commotus," GELBS said, and then in a rush of wind, she was gone.

Commotus followed her path until he was sure she had arrived safely, before turning to look at the fox. The energy levels he'd been giving off had come dangerously close to those which all the spirits had held before he'd deleted himself from their memories. Now, however, he was as dark as the rest of the creatures.

The sheer level of emotion he'd felt from his creature had been surprising. It was almost as if he'd nearly remembered his creator, and had then forcibly forgotten. If anything, that proved that the particles worked. Memories of past lifetimes, Commotus decided, were a useful way of keeping the spirits of his creatures' safe from remembering him.

Thus was the creation of dreams.

The Mystery of the Paperclip

William had been sleeping ever since she'd made the glowing particles for the creatures who lived with her, and had been planning on staying asleep until much, much, later that year. Alas, the water god had no such luck.

"William, William! Come look at this!" A whale called excitedly just before it barreled into her.

"What is it, Tim?" she asked, her words distorted by a large yawn.

"Silly William, you know my name is *Jim*, not *Tim*," the young whale laughed.

"Oh, yes, of course. How silly of me to have forgotten," William said. After uncoiling her long, serpentine body and getting a good stretch, she turned her triangular head towards the small creature. "So, what is it that you want me to come look at?"

"Oh! Right! Well, when everyone woke up this morning, it was just *there*, and we have no idea where it came from or what it is. So, we got you, because you're the oldest one here."

"What does it look like?" She called ahead as she

moved sluggishly after the overly excited whale.

"I don't even know how to describe it! It's bendy, and shiny, and-" Jim's voice cut off as he shot to the surface for a breath of air. William waited, bemused, until he came rocketing back down to her level. "-and I *really* want you to see it."

"Lead the way," the water god said, wondering what this new thing could possibly be.

The "thing" was a paperclip.

"Are you sure this is the mysterious object you needed to show me?" William asked as she stared at the massive piece of metal.

"Yes! What is it?"

"Well, it's a paperclip," William said. She wasn't exactly sure what to tell the creatures; they wouldn't know what paper was all the way down here.

"I see!" said Jim the Whale. "Hey, everyone, it's a paperclip!"

A chorus of "Ohhhh," rose from the water creatures.

"William, what does a paperclip do?"

"It is an object used to hold bigger, flatter objects together," the water god explained.

Again, there was a round of "Ohhhh."

"Have you seen one before?" Jim asked as he wiggled in excitement.

"Yes, I have, Tim, but not for a very long time."

"My name is Jim."

"Right, sorry." William looked at the large object in confusion. "I'm not sure what it's doing here, though. I haven't seen it in a few hundred million years."

The Mystery of the Paperclip

"Do you think it fell in here from out of the water?" Asked a pufferfish.

"I'm not sure exactly what caused it to land here. I'm going to go ask around about it." William began an ascent to the top of the water. "Oh," she called back down to the creatures, "Don't touch it – it might be dangerous."

"Commotus," she called as soon as she reached air.

"William! I haven't seen you in a long while. How are you?"

"Well, tired, for one. I have a question, though: Do you remember the paperclip we saw once a long time ago?"

"Yes, of course. It was really quite nice. I invented it on another planet and brought it back here when that galaxy was, ah, accidentally destroyed. Why do you ask?"

"Because it's shown up in my – I mean, your – ocean."

"That can't be right! I saw it just recently, and it told me it had no plans of going into water," Commotus said.

"Do you think it lied?" William asked.

"Well, I don't see a reason why it would- how big would you say it was, exactly?" Commotus asked.

"I'd say it was about three feet long," William replied. "Why?"

"Oh."

"Commotus? What do you mean, 'oh?'"

"Oh, nothing, don't panic or anything. It's just a little bit smaller than when I, um, originally made it." At that moment, the god of creation was thankful for the colorful cloak he was wearing, as it shielded his troubled expression from the water spirit.

"Smaller? You mean it's changing all by itself?" William didn't like the sound of that. "How can it change itself without being a god of creation, like you?"

There was a moment of silence before Commotus began speaking. "William, I think I should tell you a bit more of the story. I said that the paperclip's world was destroyed, correct?"

"Yes, Commotus, but how does that relate to it changing itself?"

"Please do not panic when I tell you this, William. It happened a long time ago, and no one is in any danger. But, well, the planet I made the paperclip on was orbiting a different black hole than the one this planet is stuck to. I was trying to spread out the creation a little bit, you know, and see how many things I could make. But, as you probably remember, the black holes were designed to trap the Maucav, or Nameless Gods, and the one inhabiting the black hole I was near was still furious with me. All of them are furious with me, actually. When I go by their black holes, I light up the inside and they remember that they aren't in the void, and that they aren't creation gods."

"Commotus, what does this all mean?" William asked, with a nervous glance back down into the water which housed all of her creatures and the paperclip.

"Right, right, sorry. The Nameless God that existed in the black hole I was playing – er, creating – near got so mad that it came out."

"It came out of the void? How is that possible?"

The Mystery of the Paperclip

William thought back to previous mentions of the Maucav. When the three elder spirits had come to the rock that was her planet, they had spoken of a mission the Maucav had given them. Had they spoken of having *seen* them, or had they just heard them? It was so long ago, the water spirit just couldn't remember.

"Please, William, stay calm," Commotus said in a low, soothing voice. "I had been near that planet for quite a while, so my light had a long time to be absorbed into it. When it climbed out of the black hole, it used up the energy I had unknowingly given it, so don't worry. You won't have to watch the skies for a super-powered attack from real gods. Anyway, in its rage, all of the planets were incinerated, and I just barely managed to get the paperclip away from its destructive power. When I brought it to this planet, I found that some of that Nameless God's energy had been imprinted onto it."

"But the Maucav don't have the ability to chance themselves, or anything else. Why is the paperclip smaller, and why is it in the ocean with the creatures I look after?"

"The thing is, I don't believe the paperclip is *changing* itself, necessarily. I believe that it is using its powers to split itself. Instead of one, big paperclip, there are two smaller paperclips."

"Does that mean the paperclip I saw is only part of the one you brought over?" William gasped.

"Well, yes. I'm still not sure what is causing the split to begin, though. Each split is an original, creative thought, and the paperclip just doesn't have the ability to do anything creative. Something external must be causing it."

"Is this something dangerous? Is it trying to make an army of paperclips?" William glanced nervously down at the water again.

"No, that I'm sure of. Every time the paperclip is divided, *all* of it is divided, including its consciousness. By the time they become numerous enough to be a threat to anything, the consciousness will have dwindled enough that they will be nearly inanimate." Suddenly, Commotus felt an icy splash of dread trickle down his back. The emotion originated from William. "What's wrong, spirit?" he asked.

"The thing that would have to touch the paperclip needs to have creative power, right?" she asked, her voice small.

"Yes, but I am the only being with creative power strong enough to do that."

"That's not true, Commotus," William whispered. "When you were near the black hole, after I destroyed all of your creatures for you, something happened. You broke that Cube-"

"-And the Cube had creative power." Commotus paused for a second to process that fact, and noted the feeling of uneasiness that was slowly creeping through him. "When I destroyed the Cube, it went into the spirits of each and every creature I created. Technically, that means I gave them the power of creation, even if only a small piece of it."

"Would a creature have enough raw creative power to activate the divide?" William asked.

The Mystery of the Paperclip

"Yes, William. Any creature could split the paperclip."

Without another word, William dove back down towards the water. As soon as she broke the surface, her cries of warning died in her throat. The paperclip, at first glance, was missing. However, a closer look at the bottom of the ocean showed that it was glimmering a little too brightly to be just sand. The paperclip was everywhere!

"My creatures! Are you alright?"

"William!" Jim the Whale called as he rocketed towards the water spirit. "We've discovered a new game! I call it the 'Whoever-Can-Make-the-Paperclip-Divide-the-Most-With-One-Touch Wins!' game."

Commotus felt the relief of the water spirit as it flowed through her, and for a second, he lost himself in it. Relief was such a fun feeling, and not one he got to experience on his own very often. However, when he released the feeling and allowed William's emotions to meld back in with the rest of his creations', he found that a different emotion – one of his *own* emotions – remained. It occupied the space just above where his heart would have been, if he had been made of flesh. The emotion was very dense, and relative to the god of creation, very small. However, for its size, the emotion was very complex. It seemed to combine the iciness of helplessness, the sharp barbs of guilt, and the leaden weight of guilt.

For a moment, Commotus ignored the feeling, and the knowledge that caused it. He nearly brought back the happiness William was currently experiencing, or the elation *Whoosh* was feeling as he soared and looped endlessly through the sky, but stopped. Commotus was a *god* – he shouldn't have to draw from the emotions of his creations, right? And yet, he knew that their happiness wouldn't be able to keep him away from his own emotions. William's happiness came from the knowledge that the creatures of earth were safe, and Commotus was glad as well. However, the paperclip was also one of his creations, and he cared about *its* wellbeing, too.

He could feel the fractured mind of the metal being. He could feel the helpless cries of each small piece of paperclip, and he could feel the *fear* each one held. The poor thing had been split too many times to understand what was going on, and its mind wasn't strong enough to understand Commotus's mental assurances that everything was going to be okay.

Even he could not fix this. Each split was the direct result of an act of creation performed by something that was *not him*, and to undo something that had been done by another creative being would be destruction. As a being of creation, Commotus was unable to destroy – or so he'd thought. During his lengthy times away from earth during the banishment of his spirits, Commotus sometimes would drift as far away from all life as he could. During those times, the emotions of all his creatures faded away until they seemed to disappear completely. Those times had become vital in his unending search for… Something.

While he still had not found this mysterious, unknown thing, he had discovered something inside

The Mystery of the Paperclip

himself which deeply scared him: Commotus had a Reset button. He knew that he could not destroy, but a whisper from Time had provided an exception: in a case where the alternative is complete destruction, the Reset button could be used to separate all matter in the not-void into nothingness, and then reform it in a completely new way. What unnerved him the most about the Reset button was not its universe-ending implications, nor was it the fact that its glow was exactly the same as the glow Time had drawn from him when he'd first escaped Chaos. Although Commotus tried not to think about it, what unnerved him the most was that this reset button was in the shape of a cube.

Thus was the creation of paperclips.

Willow Shipperley

Why Jars Are Nearly Impossible to Open

The Human race had, since the end of the War, become distinctly different in their actions than the other creatures. They could not speak any language outside of their own, and once memory of the War had faded into legend, they began to believe that the other creatures – which they referred to as "animals" – did not speak at all. However, they still held a healthy respect for the claws and teeth which they knew to be deadly.

Commotus had been paying close attention to his Humans recently, because while he had found the reoccurring souls of some of his creatures – Tim the whale being one of them – exactly zero of the Human spirits he knew had reappeared on the planet. Of course, he did recognize many spirits who had been on Earth before, but none of his special ones. Specifically, he hadn't seen Simon. Although he didn't like to admit it, Simon was one of his favorites. Of course, there was no doubt that he loved each of his creations deeply, but there was something different about Simon, and the other special creatures. Their spirits were more colorful than the rest, and Simon had been able to *remember* him. He hadn't designed any of the spirits differently from each other; each creature had been made with the same care and attention as the one before it – why were some so different?

Before Commotus had the chance to fall too deeply into his musings, a commotion on the planet drew his attention to a civilization flourishing under Infearno's control. It seemed that the only princess in the entire kingdom was supposed to be married today to the richest man from the most powerful neighboring nation. However, the emotions Commotus was sensing from the kingdom – and especially its princess – did not match the celebratory feeling the occasion was supposed to have. Instead, there was a nearly unanimous fear coming from the citizens of the main city surrounding the castle.

Commotus's first thought was that Infearno was trying to take over the world, and he was surprised to find that the Spirit was nowhere to be seen. In fact, none of the Spirits were in the area at all, which made this a completely Human matter.

"You know, if the Emperor hadn't been appointed by God, I would think he's gone mad trying to make this work," one Human said to another as they walked toward the castle in the center of the large city.

"I agree. That other country is going to completely swallow us! It's more of a non-violent takeover than a merger." The second Human glanced up at the sky with a frown, and for a moment Commotus thought that that he was looking directly at *him*. It was with mixed relief and disappointment that he realized the Human's gaze was actually fixed on the sun.

"What do you think the princess feels about all of this?" The first Human asked.

"I'm not sure. The only times we've ever been allowed to see her have been at formal ceremonies – I don't even know her favorite color!"

"Do you think she'll follow in her father's footsteps?"

The second Human frowned again. "I don't think she'll be as ruthless as he is, but I'm not so sure that's a good thing."

"I think she could be pretty ruthless if she wanted. That kind of stuff is hereditary, right?" the first Human asked. The second did not have time to reply, because at that moment they reached the castle.

"Do you have formal invitation to this God-sent marriage?" asked one armor clad guard.

"Oh, yes, hold on," the second Human said, rummaging through the folds in her tunic before pulling out a thick square of parchment. "I'm the Duchess, and this is my escort."

The guard took the card and examined the handwritten lettering for a few silent moments before nodding and handing the card back to the pair. "You will be directed to your seats inside the gates. May God shine on you."

The two Humans nodded at the guard and stepped into the large open courtyard of the castle. The reedy sound of flutes drifted through the air, mingling with the chatter of the Humans within.

Leaning close to the Duchess, the first Human whispered, "Do you see any people from the other countries?"

"Well, I haven't spent much time with the royalty of other countries, since I left to become a scribe. You can't miss them if you see them, though. They live rather far away from God, so its golden rays have not blessed their skin. You'll see what I mean." A man in an orange dyed tunic stepped up to the pair.

"I will lead you to your seats," he said with a smile. The Duchess and her companion followed him dutifully, sitting on the long stone bench where he gestured.

"You can tell that he works for the Emperor because of the color he is wearing. The royal family, as I'm sure you know, are the only ones allowed to wear yellow, because it is God's color. The servants and workers who remain inside the castle walls at all times wear the colors which are most similar," the Duchess said, gesturing to the people around them who were still milling.

"Right, yeah. I learned that in school." Pausing for a moment, her companion frowned. "Why isn't this a public ceremony?"

"Oh, it is a public ceremony. Well, parts of it are. Before the public wedding, all of the royal families are witness to the actual marriage. What everyone else sees is just for show."

"Huh," her companion said with a frown. He opened his mouth to speak again, but suddenly the ambient music cut out, and as if on cue, the sun came out from behind a cloud. Each person in the castle turned their faces to the sky, smiling as if the grace of God had just fallen on them.

Commotus was once again startled by this attention, although he realized that it wasn't *really* him they were smiling for. For a moment, he imagined that it really *was* him they were smiling at, and he allowed himself to sink into the love he felt coming from them. Sooner than he would have liked, however, the Humans turned their faces back towards the proceedings in front of them, and the feeling faded.

As the love disappeared, Commotus felt the sting of fear return sharply. What was it that was causing such an odd emotion, he did not know. He hadn't picked up anything out of the ordinary when he'd listened to the conversation between two Humans on their way to the castle. This Human tradition of marriage was something he'd come to know as a positive, happy thing. Disconcerted, he watched as the parade containing the princess's suitor reach the gate of the castle, and enter with a loud and long winded proclamation.

Quickly, they were directed by the orange and red wearing workers to the side of the courtyard opposite the royalty of the home country. Then, in an equally loud and regal parade, the princess was escorted into the courtyard from some unseen pathway farther inside the castle.

Six guards each accompanied the suitor and the princess as they crossed to the center of the courtyard, standing directly in the light of the sun. As a third man approached the pair, holding in his hands a heavy wax candle in a decorative glass jar, Commotus felt the fear of the Humans sharply escalate.

"This candle, like all others, is sacred in both of our countries, as it contains the very essence of God when it is lit. By lighting this candle together, under the full light of our God in the sky, your marriage will be blessed and our two countries will be united as one. Both of you have holy sticks which you have been hand carving under the light of the moon, and which for the first time today will be revealed to the light of the sun. Please, retrieve them now." The man paused as the princess and her suitor both turned to their guards and pulled out long wooden wands, slick with incense. "If it is now your will to complete this ceremony, you will please light your holy sticks, and then together light the candle."

A tangle of emotions pulsed through Commotus with those words, and none of them were positive. Mixed with the fear which was already present were sadness, reluctance, and anger. These new feelings were not centered in the general population, however. Instead, they were centered on the princess. The levels of fear dropped significantly when the princess lit her wand, and as the two carefully carried their flames to the candle, anticipation rose to take its place.

Just before the wands lit the candle, Commotus felt one emotion rise above the others. The princess looked up at the sun, unshed tears in her eyes, and Commotus felt what he himself had buried deep within his cosmic body. It took strength he hadn't known he'd had to focus

Why Jars Are Nearly Impossible to Open

on what was happening on his planet instead of curling up into a tight ball and allowing himself to drift through the not-void. Hopelessness. The princess seemed to be looking right at him, right through him, and all he could hear and feel from her was hopelessness. *I am alone*, she seemed to say. *There is no one to help me, and I am all alone.*

"You are not alone," Commotus growled, baring his teeth at the first planet he'd created. "You may not be able to see me, or know me, but you are never alone." Without even bothering to speak to the Spirits, Commotus pulled all the clouds from around the world and placed them between the ceremony and the sun. Ignoring the cries of alarm from the Humans in the castle, Commotus desperately searched for a way to stop the ceremony for good. The god of creation was moving so quickly that the princess hadn't even had time to blink yet, but he knew that it wouldn't be enough time to explain what was going on to Infearno.

Desperately, he began a search for someone, anyone who he could communicate through. Then, the Duchesses companion stood up. "Commotus," she said.

Commotus froze. This Human knew him? "Who are you?"

The Duchesses expression did not change as she spoke. "There is no time for questions – this body was not meant to have multiple spirits in it. Just know I am here to help you."

Commotus was speechless for a moment. A human was talking to him, and it had more than one spirit? "Please, seal the jar before the ceremony can be completed," he squeaked out.

"Of course," the Duchess said, and very slowly, she began to walk towards the ceremony. For a moment, Commotus thought that she would never get there in time, but then he realized that all of the other humans were moving in extremely slow-motion. What was going on?

When the Duchess reached the Princess and her suitor, she very calmly took the jar from the orange-clad man standing between them, and in one blindingly swift movement, twisted on the lid. For good measure, she snapped the two lit wands and extinguished their flames, and then moved back to her place in the crowd. Those around her still had their faces turned to the sky, features morphed into matching expressions of horror at the disappearance of their God.

Commotus stared in wonder as all of his creatures moved in slow-motion. Was this the doing of the being who had miraculously appeared when he needed it to? He was so used to passing through time quickly; the individual lives of his creatures blended into each other in a single, sweeping river of emotion and sound. Everything was moving so slowly now that it was almost as if time had stopped completely. Captured in the air were water droplets from a fish's tail flick, stretching up behind a stampede was a cloud of orange-red dust, poised in a large green field were two Human armies in the midst of their first charge. It was a completely different world.

"What did you do?" Commotus whispered. A small voice in the back of his head whispered that this power over time was not something he had. Was this another god?

The being in the Duchess's body looked up at the god of creation with an almost bored expression. "I stretched out time a bit so that I could do what you asked. It isn't dangerous, if that's what you're wondering."

"Is this permanent? Will everything always be so…"

"Slow?"

"Clear. I haven't seen everything like this for a very long time. It's so quiet." Commotus looked over the earth once more. The droplets had begun their journey back into the pond, the dust was beginning to slowly settle, and the first blood of battle was pouring from a mortal wound, soon to touch the ground.

The Duchess frowned. "It is not permanent, but it can stay this way for as long as you'd like."

"Keep it like this, forever. I want to always be able to see everything this clearly."

"Commotus, it isn't a good idea. Whatever feeling it is that you're trying to prolong won't last. It will fade, and you will be left searching for a way to get it back."

"How would you know this? I don't even know what you are – did I create you?"

"We have already had this conversation, Commotus," the Duchess said. As she spoke, small cracks began to form around her mouth and eyes.

"Time?" Commotus asked. He almost didn't want to be right; the spirit-turned-god only seemed to show up when something big was happening, like the god of creation getting stuck in Chaos, or discovering that he had a Reset button which was identical to the cube he'd found in a black hole.

"Correct." The cracks around the Duchess's mouth and eyes became larger, and more appeared on her hands.

"Spirit, you don't fit inside the human body. You are killing her," Commotus said.

"It was necessary. I want this to be a long-lasting universe," Time replied. Pieces of the Duchess began to flake off, and black smoke began to slowly rise out.

"What does that have to do with anything? Get out of that human before you destroy her."

"If I hadn't stepped in and sealed the jar, you would have tried to do it yourself. Your creatures would have seen you, and it would have led to the destruction of the universe."

"How could you even know that?" Commotus cried, uneasiness amplifying his distress.

"I have seen it happen before," Time said. More pieces of the Duchess broke off, and more smoke billowed out of her.

Commotus did his best to ignore the implications of Time having seen this scenario before. "You need to get out of her now, before I force you out."

"Wait," Time said. "I need to ask you something first."

When the spirit did not continue, Commotus sighed. "What is it?"

"Do you feel loved?"

Whatever Commotus had been expecting, that

Why Jars Are Nearly Impossible to Open

wasn't it. Love? What a silly question, of course he felt loved. It didn't even matter that those he loved the most had no idea if he existed, and would probably explode if they even had even the slightest understanding of who he was, but sure, he felt loved. He had the adoration of the Spirits, didn't he? And the Nameless Gods certainly wouldn't be so passionate in their anger if they didn't love him, right? Slowly, the feeling that he was missing something returned. The god of creation felt his face fall into a small frown. "What kind of question is that, Time?" he asked in a small voice.

Time looked up at him through the Duchess, and Commotus could have clearly read the pity on her face, even if he hadn't been able to feel the spirit's emotions anyway. "I'm sorry, Commotus. I really thought that this was it."

"That this was what?" he asked.

"That this was the universe where you would remember – never mind. We'll get there eventually," Time said with a sigh.

"Wait, remember what? Time, what do you know that you're not telling me?"

"I can't explain this to you. You're not ready. However, I am not going to see you again for a very long time, so I will leave you with this: you are more similar to your creatures than you think. Just as they think they are the supreme beings of their world, so do you think you are the supreme being of yours. Goodbye, Commotus. I will return when you need me most."

Before Commotus could call for Time to wait, the

Duchess crumbled to pieces on the ground and black smoke swirled in every direction. It briefly concentrated around the jar, sealing it permanently, and then it was gone. The world returned to its normal speed, and Commotus was suddenly jolted by the shock and fear of the humans, and the gratitude of the Princess. No one noticed the disappearance of the Duchess, not even her escort.

When it was found that the jar could not be opened, the king declared that no jar should ever be easy to open again, so as to appease God.

Thus no jar was ever easy to open again.

Why History Books Don't Include the Spirits

As the latest century came to a close, Commotus cheered silently. Other than a particularly extravagant attempt to take over the world – courtesy of Infearno – the past one hundred years had been somewhat boring. Of course, there were the ups and downs that came with the antics of his creatures, but the normal, everyday events of their lives had long since blurred into one long, never-ending stream. It was because of this that Commotus decided he'd been hovering around Earth for much too long. Maybe if he were to have some time to drift through his universe, without the constant buzz of other creatures' thoughts and emotions, he could come back with a fresher perspective.

In any case, as soon as the final celebrations ended and the contagious thrill of the New Year began to die down throughout the solar system, Commotus began drifting. He took special care to avoid staying near any one black hole too long, for fear of accidentally giving a Nameless God a taste of his power. Thoughts of the paperclip and its fate still sent guilt shivering through him. There was no way he was going to let another one of his creatures suffer a similar fate.

Finally, he came to a place that surpassed even the most far out galaxies. After an expectant pause, during which Commotus searched his mind for the thoughts and emotions of those other than himself, he relaxed. He was alone.

"I'm alone! For the first time since I created light, I am alone! My thoughts are my own, and my emotions are my own!" Commotus did a loop-de-loop in the not-void, feeling free in his movements for the first time. There was no worry that he would accidentally smack a solar system or two out of place, or that one of his creatures might be able to hear his laughter. "Hello," he called out joyfully, "I am Commotus, the god of creation, and I am *alone!*"

A few loops and spins later, Commotus' laughter began to die down. Almost as if a weight had been dropped into him, he felt his giddiness slip away, leaving him rather empty. "I am alone," he said again. All of a sudden, being by himself with his emotions didn't seem like the bright idea it had before. "Why am I here?" he shouted out to the not-void. It did not reply.

As he opened his mouth to shout again, a colorful beam of light reaching from the other side of the universe nearly knocked the wind out of him. "Commotus! Commotus!" sounded the panicked voices coming from the light. "Please come home, we need you!" The voices were distorted as if they were underwater, but the sudden

Why History Books Don't Include the Spirits

wave of emotions that accompanied them was not.

"What is going on?" Commotus gasped.

"Please come home!" The voices cut off suddenly, as did the light. Commotus was left drifting through the not-void for a few moments before he came to his senses.

"Was that the signal?" Commotus thought back thousands of years to the creation of the pyramids. "It has to be." After a deep breath, which was more to calm himself down than out of necessity, he began his return journey to Earth. Making it back in half the time it took to leave, Commotus looked around his galaxy in a panic. All of his planets appeared to be okay. Air traffic between solar systems seemed to be normal, and everyone's emotions were rather pleasant. Had he been wrong about the signal? Locating Earth, Commotus came to a stop.

"William, are you there?" Commotus waited expectantly, but received no reply. "Infearno? *Whoosh?* GELBS? Is anyone there?" Again, silence. Feeling more and more nervous, the god of creation looked closer at his favorite planet. Signs exclaiming "Welcome to the Year 42,000,023" and other similar sentiments flashed brightly all around.

"I've only been gone for twenty three years, and the message shouldn't be old at all. What happened?" Commotus tried to sort through the emotions of his creatures, hoping that maybe they would give him a clue as to what had transpired. However, the more he dug into the feelings, the more he realized something was very wrong with them. First off, unlike the woven and knotted masses of consciousness that he was used to, this feeling seemed to be smooth and singular. There were no fluctuations, no singularity, and no thought. Peering at the people of the planet, he noticed that even their movements were off. Unlike the flowing, organic movements he had designed his creations to use, the creatures on Earth were moving in long lines, with restricted, jerky movements.

"Who did that to you?" he murmured. Moving on to the other planets in the solar system, he discovered the same inorganic movements and emotions. After swiftly examining each planet in his galaxy, Commotus came to the conclusion that he had no idea what was going on. Just as he was about to return to Earth and try to contact his spirits again, he felt a change in the emotions. It was such a small blip that if the emotional state of the rest of his galaxy hadn't been so stagnant, he could never have noticed it. At any rate, that small blip was a shout to him.

Focusing on the small bit of emotion, Commotus tried to single it out, and tracked it down to one planet. "Little creature, who are you?" he whispered. Nervousness prevented him from speaking too loudly, as if the volume of his voice would decide whether or not his creature would be able to stand Knowing Commotus.

"My name on this planet is Ch'ill, but my true name is Simon," a small voice replied a few minutes later.

Commotus felt his eyes widen in a moment of glee. "Simon? Is that really you?"

"Well, I don't know who else I would really be. You seem familiar, voice. Do you have a name?" Simon replied.

Why History Books Don't Include the Spirits

"I am Commotus, god of creation."

"Oh, not another one. If there are so many 'gods of creation,' then why has nothing new been created since before I was born?"

The brief shot of excitement Commotus had felt at finally finding his favorite creature dimmed. "What do you mean, 'so many gods of creation?' I am the only god of creation."

"Yeah, you and everyone else."

"Can you tell me why everyone is so robotic? It looks like I picked the worst possible time to take a break."

"Well, you and your buddies are taking over the universe, and in order to stop opposing forces from growing against them, they took away Free Will."

"Yet you remain untouched," Commotus breathed. "Has anyone else escaped these other gods?"

"As far as I know, I am the only one," Simon replied curtly. "How come you don't know all this already? Don't all of you creation gods exist as some sort of hive-mind?"

"Well, like I said. I'm the only real god of creation." Commotus knew that these other "gods" had to be the Maucav, but there was no way they could have escaped. Not without the aid of some kind of creation power. He'd been exceedingly careful when passing the black holes which served as void-like prisons for the lesser gods, which meant it wasn't *his* power which had caused their collective escape. "Do you have a plan for stopping the other gods, or for waking up more people?"

"Why would I tell you that?" Simon asked.

Commotus sighed. "How do you know that your true name is Simon?"

"Well, I'm not sure. It just sort of feels right."

"I discovered your true name. I focused myself completely on your soul, and I discovered that you are Simon. It was back when I was able to talk to you and all other creatures openly."

"That's a nice little tale, but I really don't believe it."

"Simon, you are my messenger. I need you to believe me." Commotus waited for a reply, but none came. "Could you at least tell me what happened to my Spirits?"

"All three of them were destroyed, by you and the rest of the gods."

Shock briefly rendered Commotus silent, before confusion muddled the feeling. "Which three were destroyed?"

"The only three – *Whoosh*, Lux, and Sonus. You gods took them out before they could do anything to fight back. Not that they could have fought back anyway – the gods are huge!"

"What about the three created from the elements of Earth? Surely you've heard of that planet, even from all the way over here."

"There were only three spirits," Simon said. Although Commotus could not see him, he could tell that his creature was speaking through clenched teeth.

"Please, I need to know if Infearno, William, and GELBS are safe," the god of creation pleaded. He knew that if he were speaking to any other person, and if he was any less desperate for information on his longest standing companions, his anger and pride would not have allowed him to beg.

"You know their names?" Commotus sensed surprise and caution in Simon, and knew that this was his chance to convince the creature that he truly was the one god of creation.

"Of course. They named themselves just after their creation." Nervous that too much information would make him look like a liar, he kept silent about the details of his ancient memories.

"Who created them?" Simon asked, and Commotus felt a dual spike of hope and suspicion.

"Well, I guess technically I did, but I didn't mean to. I was forming the elements that exist on Earth – which was just a rock when I started – and they sort of popped up. They represent the elements, in a way."

Simon let out a breath he hadn't known he'd been holding. "I'm sorry for the way I acted. When I heard your name, I just couldn't believe it was true."

"You couldn't believe that what was true – that I really existed?"

"I couldn't believe that you weren't dead."

"Simon, as far as I know, I cannot die." Commotus paused for a moment, then continued, "Can you tell me where my Spirits are now?" Before the creature could reply, Commotus heard the wailing and shouting that signaled the arrival of the Nameless Gods.

"You!" One shrieked. "We have beaten you!"

"We are bringing back the void!" another cackled.

"We have taken back the spirits of the things which

you have created!" a third crowed.

"Behold," they spoke as one. "The Spirits of Light, Sound, and Air!"

Before Commotus could react, his three eldest spirits – miniscule in comparison to the Nameless Gods – were devoured. At once, the not-void was plunged into darkness, taking all sound and air with them. It was an impressive imitation of the void, but of course, it wasn't quite there yet.

Although Commotus could exist quite well in this environment, he knew that his creatures could not. Their collective panic, sounding from all across the universe, broke through the placid, flat feeling that had been distracting Commotus before. All of his beautiful creatures were going to die! What a painful death this was going to be, and unlike the time when he'd flooded Earth to save his creatures, he could not comfort them. Truly, this was the end.

A pressure change in the air signaled the arrival of Time. "Commotus," it said, resonating voice breaking through although Sonus was no more, "Your time here is coming to a close."

"What do you mean?" Commotus asked, dread weighing him down.

"You have a choice here. Either you let everyone die in this almost-void, or you reinvent light, sound, and air and hope the Nameless Gods don't kill everyone anyway." Neither of these choices seemed particularly inviting to Commotus.

"Is there nothing else I can do? No way to end the

Why History Books Don't Include the Spirits

suffering of all my creatures peacefully?"

"Well, you could always Reset the Universe." As Time spoke, the Cube inside Commotus's chest began to glow, illuminating a frozen scene of horror on all the planets in his vision.

"You said that if I Reset, I won't remember anything. What's to say that I won't make the same mistake next time?"

"I have seen innumerable universes, and not once has there been a repeat," Time said.

"What happens to the creatures?"

"They will become the building blocks for the next universe, just as they have in each cycle."

"What will happen to my Spirits?"

"The ones who were eaten will become energy for the Nameless Gods next time."

"What about the God of Everything Living and Beautiful and Stuff, William, and Infearno? They weren't eaten!"

"They will become Nameless Gods," Time replied simply.

Commotus felt as if he'd been punched in the gut – metaphorically, since of course he didn't have any guts. "Will they remember me?" he whispered.

"Only as much as you remember them."

Commotus felt sick at the realization that the mindless, hateful Nameless Gods used to be close companions of his. Could he really do it again? Why had he done it so many times in the past? Thinking of his creatures, though, he knew that he needed to end their pain. "How do I activate the Cube?" he whispered.

"Accept that this is only one turn in a cycle that is never-ending," Time said.

So Commotus closed his eyes, and imagined what his past universes could have looked like. In the first cycle, he was probably all alone – no Nameless Gods to scream at him. Was he always alone? It seemed like it. Yet, the Cube in his chest, and the one he had found in the black hole so long ago, were not his creations. Could it be that he was just a creature in some other, bigger God's cycle? He didn't know this time around, but maybe he figured it out in a past cycle – maybe he would figure it out in his next cycle.

"I am Commotus, god of creation," he began, "And I am ready to start over."

There was a great swell of light from the Cube in his chest, and it lit him up from nose to tail until he himself was blinded. He closed his eyes, took a deep breath, and waited.

Thus was the End of the Universe.

The Beginning of Everything

Before there was everything, there was nothing. Actually, that's not true – there was Commotus. So, before there was everything, there was exactly one thing. Although, if you were to count all of the *other* stuff in the void, there would be a lot of things. Everything, practically. However, in the darkness of the void, Commotus was the only *visible* thing, since he glowed, and therefore he was the only thing in existence.

In the end, it doesn't really matter what exactly was in the void, because it seemed that in the same instant the void came into existence, Commotus invented light, and then all of a sudden everything existed. Or maybe he waited a while beforehand, doing who knows what. There's no real way to tell, since he didn't create time until after light, but that's beside the point.

The problem with everything *not* existing and then existing all at once is that, well, everything is existing. At the same time. Even though "everything" consisted of only the Nameless Gods and himself, the dizzying cocktail of rage, fear, and longing rolling off of them was quite clear to Commotus. Although he'd never experienced any emotions like that before, they did not debilitate him. It was almost as if he'd had an unfathomable amount of time to experience and get to know them, but of course Commotus knew that he hadn't. The universe had only just begun, after all.

As he went through the process of creating things, like sound, air, and things to stand on, he could feel the jumble of emotions coming from the Nameless Gods becoming more and more tangled. However, it wasn't until he created time that they began to express those emotions outwardly.

"Take us back to the void," the howled. "Turn off the light!"

Commotus could do neither of those things, as they would involve destruction, but he still felt bad. Briefly, he considered coming up with some sort of mini-void simulation to appease them, but something inside of him knew that it was only a temporary solution. If he was going to truly help the Nameless Gods, he would have to figure out the cause of their emotional turmoil and address *that*.

"Take us back to the void," they cried again.

There was no way they could understand that he couldn't just "take them back to the void." The idea was too large for them; it wouldn't fit inside their bodies. Why did they want to go back, anyway? There wasn't anything in the void; it was dark, and soundless, and lightless, and isolated. Commotus could feel the loneliness buried underneath their rage and fear, so why would they want to be isolated?

"Take us back, take us back," they chanted. Slowly,

The Beginning of Everything

their small forms surrounded Commotus's starry body. When he made a move to speak, however, they raised their voices to drown him out. "God of creation, we reject you!" they screeched. "We reject you, and the light that you bring, before you can reject us!"

With their words came a wall of emotion that very nearly knocked Commotus over. Yet, their emotions didn't match their speech. Although their words appeared to be fueled by rage and hate, all the god of creation felt from them was fear. From some ancient depths of his being, he recognized the intentions of the Nameless Gods. Isolation, fear, and a haste to reject something before it could hurt them? Commotus knew he'd felt this before, as impossible as that was. He'd been searching for ...something, which he'd been unable to identify at the time: acceptance. No, it was more than that. Surveying the restless mob of lonely gods, Commotus knew what he had to say.

"You are loved," he whispered. The soft glow coming from inside of him increased in strength, bathing the Nameless Gods and him in its light as relief, giddiness, and love replaced the fear, hatred, and loneliness.

Thus was the creation of the Universe.

Acknowledgements

I would not have been able to make it this far without the support of those around me. First and foremost, my teacher, Suzanne Supplee, has been indescribably helpful. Even though there were seventeen other people in the class, you still managed to sit down with me and encourage my writing. You quelled my doubts about my voice in the book, and you have encouraged me to continue writing, and making jokes.

I thank my Literary Arts classmates, for giving me tips and listening to me talk endlessly about my characters.

The beautiful cover was done by Irene Javier, for which I am unspeakably thankful.

My final thanks go to both my mother, who listened to me talk about the characters throughout many car rides and walks, and who gave me advice, and my father, who supported me in making this book emotionally and financially, and who edited my final draft in only a few days to assure me it was ready to publish.

Author's Notes

This idea came to me the summer between Junior and Senior year. I'd been trying to find something to do that I felt I'd be able to write extensively about, but nothing was catching. I was sitting on a stool at the hospital I was volunteering at, waiting for a patient to come in so I would have something to do. As I spun around on the stool, I caught a glimpse of a tree whose leaves were rustling in the wind. *"Why do the leaves fall off when it gets cold?"* The thought had only a second to rest unanswered in my mind before words like "photosynthesis" and "chloroplasts" began buzzing around. *"Yeah,"* came my mind, *"but what if that was wrong?"*

I was then reminded of a lesson I'd received in Elementary School about how people used to make up stories to explain what they did not understand. This lesson had come with one of my favorite assignments: explain how something happens in a new way. *"Hey,"* my mind spoke up, *"Why don't you do that for your Senior Thesis?"* So, I did.

On a different note, I found that the designs I'd made for my characters – specifically the Spirits – were a bit two dimensional, as I had been trying to emulate the style of ancient mythology. Inspiration came from my mother, whose explanation of how the elements have been based off of emotional traits in some cultures inspired me.

Inspirations aside, my main goal in writing is to share emotion. Whether you, as the reader, found joy and love in my words, or simply thought the plot was nice, I am glad to have shared this journey with you.

About the Author

Willow Shipperley is a high school senior at Carver Center for Arts and Technology. When she is not writing, she can be found drawing, reading, and watching various YouTubers as well as her favorite shows. At the time of publication, she lives with her mother and step-father, but in the fall of 2015, she plans to attend University of Maryland College Park. Her more academic interests include physics, engineering, and calculus, which quite possibly will be the focus of her college career.

Thank you for reading.